A Soul Wounded,
But a Spirit Renewed

A Soul Wounded, But a Spirit Renewed

A Single's Guide to Living Saved, Sanctified, Satisfied and Single.

Lady Ivy A. Ashley

To order additional copies of this book, contact:
Xlibris Corporation
1-888-795-4274
www.Xlibris.com
Orders@Xlibris.com
21325

Contents

PART III: SATISFIED

PART IV: SINGLE

Dedications

This book is dedicated to the memory of my grandparents, Herbert Leroy and Sarah McKelvie Hayes. Thank You for instilling the values into my mother that she imparted into me which have helped to groom me into the woman of God I am today. I love and miss you dearly.

In addition, to my spiritual godmother Jessie Taylor. I miss you dearly. The three years God placed you in my life were a treasure. You imparted so much wisdom and knowledge into me; it is because of you that I realize "God is in Control." I will always cherish the memory of you and what you stood for.

Acknowledgments

First and foremost, I would like to thank God for giving me this opportunity to minister through this book. I count it a privilege to be one of your chosen and I don't take my assignment lightly. Thank you for trusting me with the priceless treasure of your anointing. You are the lover of my soul.

To my mom, Essie Ford, I can never repay you for all the things you have done for me. You have always sacrificed your needs and desires for me, Terrie and Howard. God has a staggering blessing waiting on you, girl! I love you madly! To my sister and brother, Terrie (Michael) and Howard (Valeta), thank you for loving and supporting me in everything I do. To my nieces and nephew Terica, Keenan and Kerrington Ivy, Auntie loves you. To my father, James Ashley and to all of my family, especially Auntie Gwen, Auntie Betty, Lisa (Tony) and Peter, thank you all for believing in my abilities. To my extended families: The Salary's, Sharpe's, Byrd's, Dickerson's, and the Orton's, thank you all for your love and concern. You all hold a special place in my heart.

It would take more space than what I have to thank all of the people who have in some way touched my life. So, if I don't mention you now, look for your name in the next book. To my friend for life, Rakisha Pickett you are very special to me. We have been through a lot together and our friendship has stood the test of time. There is nothing I wouldn't do for you, within reason, of course! To Julian, Tanya and Elgin—we will minister together again! Thank you for having my back in the realm of the spirit! To Pastors Clark and Diane Lazare, thank you for all you

9

have imparted into me, as a couple and as individuals. You are truly a blessing! To Dameon, Hi-Yah, Shammah! Thank you for being there for me, I love you like my brother! To Nikkie, Katrina J., Raymond, Celora, Joya and Erica F.—thank you for also having my back! I love you all. To my spiritual mothers, Pastor Zelma Dickerson and Rosalee Miller, thanks for being the anointed wise women you are. I truly thank God for you. To Elder Joycelyn Johnson, the woman who has been assigned with the tedious task of mentoring me—Smile! I love you for who you are and all you do. To the Servants In Ministry (SIMIN), let's take it to the next level! Tracie, thank you for your awesome administrative capabilities and your attentive ear—you are the BOMB!

To all of the ministries that have had a significant role in my spiritual life: Philippian Community Church, the late Pastor L.C. Callahan; Watson Temple C.O.G.I.C.; the late Bishop E.L. Sheppard; Mt. Calvary Baptist Church, Pastor John A. Newman; World Harvest Church, Pastor Rod Parsley; New Covenant Believer's Church, Pastor Howard Tillman and The Potter's House, Bishop T.D. Jakes, thank you all.

To everyone who purchased this book, thank you for supporting the ministry in which God has entrusted me with. God bless and keep you as you strive to be Saved, Sanctified, Satisfied and Single!

"My heart is overflowing with a good theme; I
Recite my composition concerning the king, my
Tongue is the pen of a ready writer."

Psalm 45:1

Foreword

I am grateful to God for giving me the opportunity to share with you my views of an awesome young Woman of God, Ivy Ashley and the book "A Soul Wounded, But a Spirit Renewed". Within the pages of this book, Ivy shares her life with single Christians, young and old alike, the fact that you really can live "SAVE—SANTIFIED—SATISFIED—SINGLE". Make no mistake about it, this book will make you go "Hum", for you will discover, like yourself, she was and continues to be faced with many challenges. "BUT GOD!" Through her faith in Him, and being moved by the Holy Spirit, Lady Ivy has withstood every obstacle she has faced. So be encouraged, never give up, never give in, and for God's sake, never give out! The Holy Ghost is a KEEPER; you just have to make up in your mind that you want to be kept. One way or the other this book WILL change your life!

Elder Joycelyn Johnson
Coordinator / Consultant
The Potter's House
Dallas, Texas

SIMIN©

Introduction

How Can One Be Warm Alone?

"Fantasizing and aspiring about this thing called
Love; wondering if it could be all that I've ever
Dreamed of. Someone who will respect and
Support me through thick and thin; and who
Will remain to be my sweetheart until the very
End."

Is it really possible for an individual to experience warmth as a single? Is it feasible to believe that total fulfillment can be achieved in the absence of a significant other? Most assuredly!

I must admit being a single Christian is not easy because it seems that the Church focuses more on marriage and relationships rather than contentment in holy single living. And rightly so, considering that shortly after the world began marriage was instituted in the Garden of Eden, henceforth Adam and Eve. In addition, the basis of our salvation is relationship: God loved us so much that He sacrificed a part of Himself so we could be reconciled back to Him. However Jesus, the Son of God, never married yet exhibited total satisfaction in doing the will of His Father.

Many Scriptures in the Bible instruct us as people of God to keep the Lord as our point of focus in order to reap the bountiful benefits of being a joint heir (read Matt. 6:33 and Ps. 37:4).

15

Unfortunately, we find that one may, "first seek the Kingdom" in order for "things to be added"; or "delight in the Lord" to get the "desires of the heart".

It is very normal to desire companionship; and to be honest, spending time with your brothers and sisters in the Lord may get real old. Amen somebody! Nevertheless, being single is not an abnormality; it is the time set apart for God and His will to take precedence over everyone and everything else in our lives. Genuine fulfillment is only found in an active, not a Sunday only, relationship with the Lord.

> "Again, if two lie down together, they will keep warm;
> But how can one be warm alone? Though one may be
> Overpowered by another, two can withstand him. And
> A threefold cord is not quickly broken."
> Ecclesiastes 4:11-12

When you try to handle your singleness on your own, disaster results because your actions are flesh led and not God led. Once you allow yourself to experience Godly love, you will not be tricked by a cheap imitation. You will realize that while you maybe alone, you are never lonely because God fills in all those empty places. When you come together with the Lord, you can withstand anyone and anything. In His divine timing, He will release unto you your mate, which will form that threefold chord that is not quickly broken.

In the following chapters, we will take a close look at how one can begin to live saved, sanctified, satisfied and single. First, we will look into how to form and establish an intimate relationship with the Lord, so that He can reveal His divine purpose for our lives. Then, we'll look at what the word sanctification really means and how being sanctified can aid us in living a victorious Christian life as a single. Next, we will get an understanding of what it means to lose ourselves in the Lord and allowing His agenda to become our very own. Finally, we will explore and define the topic of single-hood and discover how we can obtain total satisfaction and contentment in this state.

The Lord sent me to be an encouragement to you. In spite of what people may have said, you can be single and live holy. If you are only 50% or 75% of a person, another half or quarter will not make you a whole! Until we are satisfied in our relationship with the Lord, God will not send a mate in our direction because we need to understand what the true purpose of a spouse is. Marriage is a ministry, not just sex!

I know your struggle because I am there! I am not a married person trying to give single people advice. I am single too! As you read this book, I pray that you find encouragement and complete deliverance in your life as a single.

PART I

Saved

"I Now Yield"

You've supplied my every need; You've blessed me when
    I ignored Your call,
No matter what You did for me, I refused to give You my
    all.
But now my eyes are opened, I want to do Your will,
Lord, hear my earnest plea, to You I want to yield.

I rendered myself to the flesh for so long, until I am
    ashamed,
But Lord I now realize that being saved is no game.
I repent unto You in sincerity, so on my knees I kneel,
To your every word, I want to yield.

When I submit myself to God, the devil will have to flee,
For greater is He that is living on the inside of me.
I can't live without You any longer, my heart has been
    filled,
To your every call, I want to yield.

I keep asking myself, "Why did you wait so late?"
But Lord, you knew exactly what it would take.
I now know that my deliverance has completely taken
    place,
And now I can with whole-heart run this Christian race.

I refuse to be tricked by the enemy from this day forward,
you no longer have a place in my life,
So be dismissed all afflictions, persecutions, envy and
strife.
Lord I am ready, send me to work in your fields,
I thank You for Your unmerited favor, to You "I Now
Yield".

Chapter One

In the Beginning

" . . . because God from the beginning chose you
for salvation through sanctification by the Spirit
and belief in the truth" (II Thess. 2:13).

For as long as I can remember, I have enjoyed writing
everything from poetry to short stories. However, when God
instructed me to begin writing a book geared towards single
women I panicked! I mean, what could I possibly say that
would help someone in his or her singleness, seeing that I
was not content in my own single state. Well as I later
discovered, God calls us because He knows where we will be
in the future; it is us who linger on who we are now. This book
was initiated back in 1996 and this is 2003; God had me
endure seven years worth of preparation and women of God,
it was quite tedious! (Note, I am still experiencing preparation!)
Nevertheless, during this time I have had some experiences
that would qualify me to write everything you are about to
read. I guarantee you will find nothing in these bounded pages
that is secondhand information. I can honestly say that as a
result of the pruning and pressing I endured, I depend on
God more and man less. For it is in Him that I am complete.
So here we go, sister to sister, single to single; my experiences
from the beginning.

During my junior year at Florida A&M University in Tallahassee Florida, I accepted my call into the ministry. While attending a Sunday night service at the church I was a member of at the time, one of the missionaries was speaking on getting rid of your excuses when it comes to doing what God has called you to do. At this point in my life I found myself feeling like the Prophet Jeremiah:

> "Then said I: Ah, Lord God! Behold, I cannot
> speak, for I am a youth.' But the Lord said to
> me: Do not say, I am a youth; for you shall
> go all to whom I send you, and whatever I
> command you, you shall speak. Do not be
> afraid of their faces, For I am with you to
> deliver you, says the Lord" (Jer. 1:6-8).

I guess being young in age and not well versed in Scripture would have been my excuses. However, the Lord let me know that when I depend on His strength in my weakness I could not fail. Ministry requires total dependence on God and submission to His will. A call into ministry requires an appointing and then an anointing. Just because God has revealed His call upon your life does not mean it is your season to come forth. Unfortunately, many men and women make the mistake of calling themselves or allowing someone to push them into a position God has not called them into. We have all been called to be ministers of reconciliation once we have accepted Jesus Christ as our Savior. The only way for man to be connected back to God is through a personal relationship. However, the call into one or more of the areas of the fivefold ministry, e.g. apostles, prophets, evangelist, pastors and teachers requires additional responsibility.

> "My bretheren, let not many of you
> become teachers, knowing that we shall
> receive a stricter judgment" (Jas. 3:1).

In essence, please make sure that you are being led by the Spirit and not a spirit! We'll discuss this topic more a little later.

After I acknowledged that God had revealed to me the call of ministry, I entered my stripping period. This is when God allowed everything in my life that was not like Him to surface so that He could clean my temple! Every thought, act, emotion and person that was not in the will of God was removed! This process can either be slightly painful or unbearably excruciating, depending on our willingness to surrender. If the truth be told, once God begins to strip us, He continues the process throughout our relationship with Him.

I was excited about God choosing me to have such an awesome responsibility. However, I didn't immediately start to run tent revivals or crusades. I wanted God's full approval of my every move, so it made sense for me to allow Him to be my guide. When the Lord saw the sincerity of my heart, the stripping process began with a dream I had one night.

The Dream

It was a Friday evening and the setting was an extravagant mansion. I can remember my friends and family being in attendance, but I can't name anyone in particular. I was about to be married the following day, so this was the rehearsal dinner. The atmosphere was like that of a fairy tale. My fiancée and I seemed to be very happy and in love. Though I don't remember his face, I can recall these attributes: Tall, dark, handsome and bald!

As the hour became late, our guest began to leave. My fiancée and I were alone in one room while two of my girlfriends were asleep in another room. As we talked and reminisced about how we met and how much we looked forward to spending the rest of our lives together, something happened. As we looked into each other's eyes we kissed, caressed and before we knew it we had consummated our relationship the night before our wedding day. (Yes ladies, this is still a dream!)

We were very remorseful and repentant to God because we had allowed the feelings of our flesh to dictate our actions. However, we did not condemn ourselves. As I prepared to leave, I asked my fiancée if he would be O.K. alone in the house; he told me not to worry for all would be well. He kissed me goodnight and I parted with my girlfriends.

Early the next morning I was awaken by a call and was informed that I needed to come back to the house where the rehearsal dinner had taken place. Without hesitation, I got dressed and went to the house. As I approached the mansion, I realized the street was flooded with police cars and an ambulance. When I arrived at the entrance of the house, I was told my fiancée had been shot and killed in a robbery attempt, on our wedding day! I cried, but for some reason they were not tears of sorrow. Weeks later, I discovered I was pregnant with his child.

After having a dream like this, I was utterly shaken. The occurrences were too real and the details were too specific for it to be just another dream. I felt I was actually living the experience. To be honest, the consummation seemed so real until I actually felt it. That really took my emotions for a loop! I spoke with a couple of my spiritual sisters and they agreed there was something more to this dream. Their advice to me was to pray and ask God for the interpretation; and that's exactly what I did.

About a week or two later while in bible study, a young lady came to me and uttered these words: "The Lord really wants to use you, but there is something in your life you need to surrender. I don't know what it is, but pray and ask God about it." Instantly, I knew what she was referring to: My secret desire to have a certain young man as my husband. However, in my mind I thought, "Lord, you know I have given him up!" In response, the Lord said, "Evidently not!" Those words hit me like a ton of bricks and I dropped to my knees and cried out to God. I began to say, "Lord, I'm sorry; he's not more important to me than You. I'll give him up for You." The more I repeated these words my spiritual man experienced an immense release. The burden I had so faithfully carried for three years had been lifted! God could've delivered me a long time ago, but I refused to give Him the situation. Sometimes we say with our mouths we have given things to God, but in actuality all we are doing is playing tug-of-war with Him. Since God is a gentleman, He will let His part of the rope go so that when we fall, we realize our need for Him. As a result, we will come to Him willingly.

When I arrived at my apartment that night, I shared with my roommate what God had revealed to me. The more we talked, the more I realized God was giving me the interpretation for the dream I had.

The Interpretation

The fact that I was to be married symbolized a very close relationship I had with someone in the natural. The presence of the wedding party, family and friends illustrated that others were aware of the feelings that existed between the two of us. The consummation was not literal; it demonstrated how God wanted me to become more intimate with Him so that my spiritual baby (ministry) could be conceived. The murder of my fiancée actually displayed God removing the natural complication, which prohibited my spiritual delivery. Since it had taken me so long to conceive God's promised seed, I could not afford any more delays toward my delivery. God will not place His seed of promise into an ill-prepared womb. At this point in my life I had chosen the perfect man for myself; for purposes of privacy, well' refer to him as 'Tim'. Tim was saved, sanctified and filled with the Holy Ghost, with the evidence of speaking in other tongues and a minister. This type of man would be any Christian woman's dream, but not necessarily in God's will for her to have. I realized later on I really didn't love Tim; I was only in love with his image. Deep down inside I knew he was not the man for me. Unfortunately, when you are frustrated with being single, you may come to the point where your flesh will lead you to accept anything that looks half way right. Can I get a witness? And if the truth be told, this leads to utter chaos!

It's Time to Get Dressed!

As I said before, it was this dream and its interpretation that led me to my stripping process. And I'm telling you, it did not feel good. Whether you agree or disagree, understand or are completely confused, God will strip you of everything that is not like Him! The process can go much easier if you submit and follow His directions. Disobedience is a no, no; it only lengthens the process and adds much chastisement to your spiritual backside.

When you enter this period of reconstruction, the very first thing God will do is show you yourself. Before He can take you to the next level in your relationship with Him, He has to deal with you where you are now! This includes your past and your present. We'll refer to this as self-examination.

> "But let each one examine his own work,
> and then he will have rejoicing in himself
> alone, and not in another. For each one
> shall bear his own load" (Gal. 6:4-5).

You may be wondering why self-examination is necessary and if you really need to take yourself through this unpleasant process. In short, if you think you have gone far beyond this type of spiritual scrutiny, it is you I am speaking to! So many times we, as people of God, get so complacent in our current states and because we've been a particular way for so long, change is heart wrenching. The most crucial aspect of self-examination is crucifying the "I" and allowing the Holy Spirit within you to stand up and take dominion in and over your life. In order for God to be the "I am" of your life, self has to die and do so daily. This process isn't an option; it is a mandate for every individual who yearns to fulfill the will of God for his or her lives. Once you enter into the perfect will of God, He will begin revealing things about you, the good, bad and the ugly, whether you like it or not! It is impossible to go to the next level spiritually and maintain with the presence of sin's residue.

Self-examination involves the following: **Realization, Filtration, Deliberation** and **Liberation.**

1. **Realization** involves the admittance of what is so that a change may take place. Our entire walk with God is contingent upon us sharing with another our belief: "For with the heart one believes unto righteousness, and with the mouth confession is made unto salvation" (Romans 10:10). While a person may believe in God and acknowledge the presence of sin in his/her life, their salvation is not sealed until a confession is made. You don't believe or think confession, you speak it!

When attending an Alcoholics Anonymous meeting, one of the first things the facilitator will tell the alcoholic is the first step to recovery is admittance. If the alcoholic never admits that there is a problem with alcohol, nothing can be done to alter the situation. Once we come to the point of realizing there are some things that dwell on the inside of us that shouldn't be, we give God the open door He needs to begin the process of self-examination.

2. **Filtration** is the act or process of purification; to be strained; to exert to the utmost (Webster 126). Purification has become a dirty word in the Body of Christ. Just because God allows us to come to Him as we are, He loves us too much to allow us to stay that way. When God looks at us, He sees us through the realm of the Spirit. That means He sees us covered with the blood of His precious Son. Hebrews 10:12&14 reads, "But this man, after He had offered one sacrifice for sins forever, sat down at the right hand of God; For by one offering He has perfected forever those who are being sanctified." The sacrifice Christ made causes us to be seen as perfect in the eyesight of God. When Jesus died on the cross, He

crucified every sin, illness, oppression, depression, hang up and downfall. Ain't God good?

In Jeremiah 18, God instructs this prophet to go down to the potter's house so that He can reveal some things to him. In researching the clay, wheel and the potter, I discovered some very interesting facts. First, the clay was a mixture of sand, dust and spittle (Nelson 19); or in layman's terms, spit! Once the clay was formed, it was walked upon by the feet of men to form a paste. After the paste was formed, the clay was placed on the potter's wheel to be shaped. The clay was then formed into a vessel by being smoothed and coated with a glaze and burned in a furnace. The vessel was then refined by fire; after which, it was ready to be presented as merchandise.

In verse 3 of chapter 18, Jeremiah says he saw the potter making something at the wheel. Even though he physically saw the potter working, he could not decipher what was being made. At times, God will do things with us that we don't understand and then continue on without explanation. This is why we must trust in Him completely and realize He knows what He is doing. The potter's clay was derived from sand and spit, nothing more and nothing less. However, what was being fashioned was much more valuable. Before God begins to mold and fashion us, we are just a lump of sand and spit. But thank God our condition is not our conclusion! What is does not affect what God says will be! Glory! The clay simply symbolizes something God can use; someone who is willing for his or her steps to be ordered by God.

As you notice, the potter did not just throw the clay on the wheel to begin molding. The clay had to be trodden upon by men. It had to be made strong by testing its durability. If the clay could withstand being trampled upon by men, surely it could endure being stretched on the potter's wheel. Ladies, if God be for you, who can be against you? Let them talk about and lie on you. While they talk, pray and seek God; don't allow people and there opinions interrupt what God desires to do in and through you. If you are doing all you know to do and you're walking

Godly, people will always find something to be critical about. Continue to do what you are doing. Speak, don't hold grudges and be petty. Kill them with kindness; it works!

In verse 4, Jeremiah says the clay was "marred in the hands of the potter". In other words, the clay became disfigured. As a result, the potter had to start over and reshape the clay. The pains of the wheel may sometimes cause us to want to move off the wheel prematurely. When we don't allow God to complete His work in us, we only become an unfinished, disfigured mound of trampled over sand and spit! Nevertheless, recognize this: Once we allow God's will to occur on the wheel, we are no longer recognized as clay but a vessel. What God allowed me to see is He cannot pour into us while we are in the form of clay. We have to allow Him to shape us into vessels so we can hold substance. But, before the vessel can hold anything, it had to be burned in a furnace! Malachi 3:3 makes reference to a refiner who is a purifier of silver. In order for the refiner to purge metals, he used fire to burn off the impurities. If the refiner did not burn his metals, they turned out to be useless. If we expect to be who God has called us to become, we must endure the heat from the fiery trials. The Scripture in I Peter 4:12 tells us, " . . . do not think it strange concerning the fiery trial which is to try you, as though some strange thing happened to you." I am here to tell you, it's not strange it's just the fire!

Filtration is not a feel good process, for you will be broken down to your least common denominator. This is crucial because God does not need any more lumpy clay. He is looking for earthen vessels to hold His priceless treasure, the oil of the Holy Ghost!

3. **Deliberation** means to weigh well in one's mind or to consider (Webster 83). This step in the process reminds me of a jury associated with a court case. Once the evidence has been presented by the prosecuting attorney, the defense and all of the witnesses have testified, the fate of the accused lies in the hands of the jury. The jury is instructed by the judge not to allow anything except what was presented in the courtroom

affect their decision. The jury is then released to weigh the evidence presented by both sides to determine whether the accused is guilty or innocent. What I find interesting about deliberations is something referred to as reasonable doubt. If the jury cannot come up with a verdict that they all agree on collectively, the verdict can be what is called a hung jury. As a result, the case is discarded, never to be tried again. It is so wonderful to know that once God purifies us by straining and exerting us to the utmost, our case has been discarded. All the evidence the devil could have used to prosecute us, has been burned by the Refiner! Praise God for the presence of the fire!

4.   **Liberation** is the act of freeing or to disengage and cut loose (Webster 197). Once we realize that God wants to do more with us and we allow Him to filtrate or separate us from the impurities that exist in our lives, we can be confident that we are free. Not free to do whatever we want to, but free to serve and do the will of the One has who sent us.

Self-examination is a very extensive process. However, if you sacrifice and allow God to thoroughly search you and be in control, He will do a great work in you! Notice that filtration is the most extensive and detailed step in the process. Purification does not happen overnight, it takes time. When you allow the master Potter to mold you into a vessel, no one will be able to conceive that you were once sand and spit. I admonish you to realize that there are some changes in your life that need to be made. Next, allow God to filter out all of the impurities, which exist on the inside of you by exerting you to the utmost. Only then will you be able to deliberate or consider the past issues that have caused you to live in a state of guilt. At any rate, once you realize "whom the Son sets free is free indeed," you can move and operate in the liberty that Jesus has provided, never to be entangled by sin again!

Questions to Ponder

1. Have I ever allowed God to take me through a 'stripping period'? If no, why not?

_____

_____

_____

_____

_____

_____

2. If yes, what did I learn about myself and God after my 'stripping period' was over?

_____

_____

_____

_____

_____

_____

3. What step(s) in the process of self-examination do I feel are most relevant to me? Why?

_____

_____

_____

_____

_____

_____

Chapter Two

Knowing God as Yah

"Behold, God is my salvation, I
will trust and not be afraid; For
Yah, the Lord, is my strength
and song; He also has become
my salvation" (Isa. 12:2).

Now that we have discovered what it takes to enter into
self-examination, there is another base we must touch. It is
very important to lay a firm foundation in God while we are
yet single. The marriage union is no place for you to figure
out who you are in God; the elementary principles should be
surpassed! In order for us really understand the art of intimacy,
we must experience intimacy with God first.

The Bible declares that the world is comprised of the lust of
the flesh, the lust of the eyes and the pride of life (see I John
2:16). Unfortunately, this concept tends to rule the life of the
unbeliever or even the believer whose mind continuously
functions in the carnal realm. Relationships among the saints
tend to be based on the attributes of the flesh because our ideals
about relationships, for the most part, were formed while we were
still in or of the world. Yes, I know you grew up going to church;
but if the truth were told, the Church was not in you. It is important
to realize carnal methods cannot be used to obtain a man or

34

woman of God. If you desire your mate to possess valor and integrity, you must know what it means to be intimate, God's way.

Divine intimacy involves a close relationship with God. In trying to find a more specific definition for intimacy, I never saw it coupled with the word "sex". The words intimacy and sex have the tendency of being used interchangeably, even though one is not contingent on the other. You can be intimate with someone without ever having sex; and likewise, you can have sex with someone without ever being intimate. Intimacy involves the connection of spirit, not body. When you focus on connecting in spirit with a man and not body, God can do so much more in the midst of the parties involved. When we become intimate with the Lord, we are able to delight in Him and Him only. Once we do this, whether or not our desires are of God is not a concern. When we are filled to capacity with Him and satisfied by Him we are truly complete in Him!

"Trust in the Lord forever, for in Yah, the
Lord is everlasting strength" (Isa. 26:4).
"Sing to God, sing praises to His name;
Extol Him who rides on the clouds, by
His name Yah, and rejoice before Him"
(Ps. 68:4).

Yah is short for Yahweh, the Hebrew word for God's personal name. It is a form of the Hebrew verb "to be" which is translated as "I am" (Nelson 823). When God revealed to Moses He had been chosen to be the vessel to lead the Israelites out of Egypt, He asked God, "Who shall I say sent me?" God's response was simply, "I am who I am; tell them I am sent me." What God was trying to get Moses to see was whatever need he had, He was able to meet that need. God has the ability to be for us whatever we need, depending on the situation. If we need provision, God becomes Jehovah Jireh. If we need peace, He becomes Jehovah Shalom. Whatever we need, God is! But, in order for us to know God as Yah, the following attributes must be present in us: Trust, Sacrifice, Uninhibited Praise and Pure Worship.

Trust denotes relationship or reliance. To trust in God means a lot more than just believing in Him. There are a lot of people who believe in God but don't live for Him. As a matter of fact, Satan believes in God! When you know God as the "I am" of your life, you depend and rely on His every word. When you are really able to trust in God, you have established a personal relationship and not just a casual acquaintance.

To sacrifice means to surrender an offering to God. An offering of what you ask? Plain and simply put, the offering is you!

> "The sacrifices of God are a broken
> spirit, a broken and a contrite heart, These
> O God, you will not despise" (Ps. 51:17).

A broken spirit and a broken and a contrite heart denote complete surrender to God. These characteristics are critical to possess in order for our praise to be uninhibited and for our worship to be pure. True enough, everything that has breath can praise God; however, all praise is not without restraint or restriction. Have you ever attended a service where it seemed there was a pull on the praise and worship portion of that service? For the most part, we neglect to consecrate ourselves before we attend church. As a result, we carry the occurrences of our day and the situations of our lives into an atmosphere that is supposed be charged with the presence of God. That is why it takes three fast songs and two slow songs before an atmosphere that is conducive for the Holy Ghost to operate in can be created. You must be willing to go beyond the realms of the familiar and what is comfortable. This is where pure worship comes in. Worship is reserved for those who know God in spirit and in truth (John 4:23-24). If you do not possess God's spirit then you cannot worship Him because you will not know what type of worship is acceptable unto Him.

When you have come to the point where you have completely dedicated your life to the Lord, being divinely intimate with Him will not be a chore but your heart's desire.

You will anticipate getting into His presence and going beyond the veil of worship instead of being complacent in the outer and inner courts of praise.

Food For Thought

As single Christians, it is imperative for us to place ourselves into a position to hear from God in every area of our lives. I know this may come as a shock to you, but God didn't save and give you purpose just for you to be someone's husband or wife. Again, there is nothing wrong with having a desire; that's not the behavior I am addressing. I am talking about those of us who are driven by the idea of marriage. For example, I think it is foolish for a woman to go pick out bridesmaids dresses and look at reception halls when there is no man in sight! Do you honestly believe that a true man of God yearns to be joined wit someone who operates in behavior that resembles witchcraft? Certainly Not!

When we allow God to be "Yah" in our lives, he fills all those voids that several intimate relationships could not touch. When we are whole in Him, we will not demand that the individuals we join ourselves with meet unrealistic expectations. When we know God as "Yah", we will understand that the purpose of marriage is ministry and our perspective spouses are only an addition to the work God has already completed!

Questions to Ponder

1. Have I taken the time to get to know God in an intimate relationship? If yes, how? If no, Why not?

_____

_____

_____

_____

_____

_____

2. Do I find it easier or more difficult to make sacrifices in my relationship with the Lord when compared to past or current dating relationships? Why?

Chapter Three

Building a House Worth Living In

" . . . and on this rock I will build My Church
and the gates of Hades shall not prevail
against it" (Matt. 16:18).

God has taught me to be a very observant person. When you
learn to look at things in the spiritual realm and not through the
eyes of the flesh, you can grasp much insight on Scripture. For
the past few years I have noticed some things in the church that
are mind boggling, but not surprising. It seems everyone feels
they have a calling to do everything but live holy! If God has
called a person to be an evangelist or an usher, it seems at the
very least they should be able to control their flesh. Once you
have formed a relationship with God and you begin to know Him
as Yah, it is normal to want to know what He has purposed for
your life. However, God is not about to implant His promised
seed into an ill-prepared body. Neither will God allow His seed
to be housed in a discombobulated building.

There are things one must do to make sure their physical body
is healthy, e.g. eating right and exercising. Likewise, our spiritual
house must incur daily maintenance to insure proper function.

House: a building or structure for the
habitation or use of man (Webster 163).

From its definition, one can gather that in order for a house to fulfill its function, someone needs to dwell in it. Imagine that you have been invited to stay with a relative or close family friend at their estate. As you drive through the ironclad security gate, you notice a well-manicured lawn, a man-made heart-shaped pond and a beautiful ensemble of roses, tulips and chrysanthemums. The house itself is nothing short of immaculate: An old English three-story split-level house with a modern flare. From the outside's presentation, you cannot wait to see the inside. Nevertheless, to your dismay, the inside of the house is nothing short of erroneous. As you enter into the foyer, you find thick clouds of dust permeating the air. The smell of mothballs and garbage is maintained throughout the house, until the very stench is embedded into the walls. Surely, the outside of this house was not indicative to what its inside contained. Unfortunately, this is how the world views the Body of Christ. We look good and shout well, but our outward appearance seems to be a contradiction to what we say is taking place on the inside. Everyone wants a title, but no one wants to be sanctified. Ask yourself this question: Is my outward appearance a demonstration or a contradiction to what I say is taking place on the inside of me? Only you and God can answer that question honestly.

Under Construction

It is detrimental that we keep our earthen vessels in check daily. The physical body is what houses the spirit man and the soul. Just as the door of a physical house protects or guards what enters in, God made the body to become a mighty fortress designed to protect the spirit. As stated before, in order for a house to fulfill its function, someone will need to dwell in it. The Holy Ghost is a person who needs a body that has been set apart to abide in. With this in mind, if He has taken residence on the inside of us, we must be conscientious that our words and actions do not grieve Him. In the next few paragraphs, you will discover a parallel between the aspects of a physical house and the parts of our body so you can better understand how detrimental it is for us to work together in the body of Christ. The body can be no better than its individual members.

The structure of a house includes the following: The foundation holds the house off of the ground and distributes the weight of the house and its contents over soil. The floors are designed to carry loads, e.g. people, furniture, bathtubs and the unexpected must all be supported without sagging, creaking, groaning or complaining. Just as the foundation supports the floor, the floor supports the walls, which support the second floor, ceiling and the roof. The walls must be placed adequately so they will yield support to all needed elements. In addition, a partition is a type of wall that separates two rooms but has no structural purpose (Jackson 30-33). The door is used as an entrance from the outside or between rooms. It is also known as an avenue or means of approach. Also, the doorknob is the instrument used to open the door by turning it to the left or to the right. The key is used for shutting or opening a lock. A window is an opening in the wall for the admission of light or air. The ceiling is the upper inside surface of a room. Lastly, the roof is the cover of any building (Jackson 152-180).

That paragraph alone will preach! Can you see where I am going with this? Let's see if your instincts are right. I promise after reading the following, you will never be able to look at a house in the same light!

Building Your Building

The foundation of a house is likened to our salvation. Our entire walk is based upon John 3:16. If you are unsure of your salvation, your foundation will not be able to support the strong meat of your faith, see Hebrews 5:12-14. In Ephesians 6, Paul talks about the helmet of salvation. The helmet of the Roman soldier was made of bronze and covered the cheeks and jawbone tightly. Inside of this helmet was a spongy like material used to protect the soldier from a possible blow by the enemy. When we are tightly secured in our salvation, people will notice and the devil will too! However, when the helmet is not on, the enemy has easy access to the elements that support our salvation. It is then he attempts to shake and/or destroy our foundation in Christ.

The feet can be compared to the floor of a house. The interesting fact about the floor of a house is it has the responsibility of carrying the weight of the entire house and its contents. If it is unable to do its job, sagging and creaking will develop. What is funny to me is the author who I assembled the previous information from said the house was to do its job without 'groaning' or 'complaining'. Initially, when I read this statement, I did not understand how a house could 'groan' or 'complain'. But think about it. Whenever you are walking, moving furniture or sitting in an edifice you may hear a small creaking in the floor or the walls. By the way an edifice is constructed, it automatically adjusts itself when new weight is introduced so that it can support the contents. When the weight of our load seems a little too heavy for us, murmuring can result.

> "Do all things without complaining and disputing,
> that you may become blameless and harmless,
> children of God without fault in the midst of a
> crooked and perverse generation, among whom you
> shine as lights of the world." (Philippians 2:14-15)

In essence, when you feel yourself about to complain, speak the word into your spirit. Don't dwell on what is; focus on what God says will be! While the weights and issues of life may cause you to question God's will for your future, His word will not return to Him void—it must accomplish EVERYTHING He intended!

The wall is used as a support system. In addition, it provides a means of protection for what is located on the inside of a house. Our body acts as a means of protection for our spirit. The spirit of God must have a body to dwell in. Even though its function is important, the body or flesh is not the dominating element. In Romans 7:18, Paul tells us that nothing good dwells in the flesh. He goes on to say, "For the good that I will to do, I do not do; but the evil I will not to do, that I practice." However, in the eighth chapter of Romans, we are charged to walk according to the spirit and not the flesh. This can only be done if we have our minds renewed and we die daily to ourselves. The "I" which includes our intellect, will and emotions must be crucified every single day. I remember the Lord saying to me, "I am about to teach your flesh how to obey your spirit." Believe me, my flesh was not trying to be trained. Everything that is contrary to the will of God is what the flesh will take delight in doing. Dying to the will of the flesh is not something you achieve; it is a continual process. I don't know about you, but I have no desire to allow my flesh and the works therein to contradict the lifestyle I am confessing to live in Christ. "But I discipline my body and bring it into subjection, lest, when I have preached to others, I myself should become disqualified" (I Cor. 9:27). One small note about the partitions: As you read, they have no structural purpose, but they aid in separation. That means that the house would be able to stand without the presence of them. As you will read later, the process of separation is not needed to make it into heaven. However, if you are not content with just being saved and want to experience the deep things of God, separation is for you.

The heart of man is where his belief in God is established. Henceforth, the door of a house and the heart of man share common ground. "For with the heart man believeth unto righteousness" (Rom. 10:10). As you will read later, the breastplate of righteousness is to be worn by every believer. It was used to protect the soldier's most precious organ, the heart. In the natural sense, if a person has the ability to get inside the door of a house, they gain access to whatever is located on the inside of the house. When we give our hearts away frivolously, we give another individual access into every area of our lives. That is why we must be very careful to whom we give our hearts to. What we fail to realize is that while it is so easy to open ourselves up and give our hearts away, it is not so easy to get them back. If the truth were told a lot of you reading this book have never recovered your heart from past relationships. That is why you may find it difficult to get into a relationship because a portion of you is still with someone else. On the opposite side of the spectrum, you may find it easy to give your heart away, because you are in search of some thing that may have been lost a long time ago! " . . . and the peace of God, which surpasses all understanding, will guard your hearts and minds through Christ Jesus" (Phil. 4:7). Allow Jesus to help you guard your heart; don't allow the feelings of your flesh to dictate to you who you should or shouldn't give your heart to.

The doorknob is what opens the door. Just as we believe with the heart, confession is made with the mouth. That brings us to that untamable, unruly evil that is located on the inside of our mouths, the tongue, which is to be associated with the key. It can be used to speak blessings and evil; it can tear a house apart or build a happy home. A key is sized to fit a particular lock, so the key to my house should not open my neighbor's door. Likewise, we should focus on taming our own tongues instead of worrying about the man next door. We should manage the key that opens the lock that is connected to our own doorknob. The thing we must realize is the Holy Spirit has given us the ability to keep this slippery, wagging piece of flesh under control! So we must decide, who will have control, the Holy Spirit or the tongue? Whichever one you find yourself feeding the most is the one who will come out as the victor!

The roof is the cover of any building; it is what people see from the outside. The ceiling is the upper inside of a room and can only be seen once the house has been entered into. We can therefore conclude that our head is like the roof of a house and our mind is like that of a ceiling. As a single Christian, our head is Christ; He's the man in our lives. I'm sure you would have preferred not to hear that statement because you have heard so many married people tell you, to allow God to be your husband or wife. Unfortunately, this is so much easier said when you have a man or woman to legally share the sheets with you at night. If the truth were told, many Christians never experienced contentment in their own singleness, but freely offer advice once they say "I do". I am just getting to the point where I am content with it just being the Lord and I. But believe me, it was a tedious task getting here and continues to be a chore staying here. At any rate, as we get to know God in an intimate relationship, He will teach us how to be single. Once we have become complete in our singleness, He will teach us how to be the wives and husbands he has designed for us to become. It is important that we allow the spirit of the Lord to govern our minds and thought patterns. That is why Romans 12:2 tells us to renew and transform our minds that we may prove what's good and perfect in the eyesight of God. It is crucial that our thoughts be placed under subjection to hear what the Word of God is saying to us.

Building a house is truly an extensive process. Did you notice that only the structural part of a house was discussed? No talk of interior decorating, laying carpet and such. That is because these are only minor details. When the structure of a house is sure, all the other elements are simple. One more note about the foundation. Construction workers don't build a house above ground. In order for a firm foundation to be produced, they must dig deep into the ground. The greater the building, the deeper they must dig because the foundation must be able to support the weight of that building. When what God has called you to do is great, He must dig deep so that you will be able to carry the weight of the anointing it takes to effectively work in your call. It may seem like everyone else is seeing their floor poured and their walls forming; you have no idea how long they have had to endure the digging process. In addition, just because a "house" is present, does not mean God laid the foundation! Remember, what God has for you is uniquely yours, and you'll receive it in due time.

Questions to Ponder

1. What part of a natural house can I most identify with? Why?

   _____

   _____

   _____

   _____

   _____

   _____

2. What parts of my "house" need to go under construction? Why?

   _____

   _____

   _____

   _____

   _____

   _____

Chapter Four

Pregnant With A Purpose

" . . . I must preach the kingdom
of God to the other cities also,
because for this purpose I have
been sent" (Luke 4:43).

Now that you have experienced or confronted self-examination, been informed on how to know God as Yah and realized there is some spiritual construction to endure, the time has come to discuss purpose. Purpose is defined as a predetermined goal or an end point of resolution. The path one takes to fulfill their purpose has already been precisely designed for the individual who must physically follow the layout. God has strategically orchestrated the road each one of us must take to get us to our destiny. This is why it is important to make sure we seek God for His will, get in His will and stay right in the center.

"Now may the God of peace make you
complete in every good work to do His
will, working in you what is well pleasing
in His sight, through Jesus Christ" (Heb. 13:20a-21)

God's will is the safest place to be but it is not the most

47

comfortable place to be. I'm sure many of you reading this book can attest to that fact! It is amazing how we can think we are pleasing God while doing what we want to do. Sometimes we can get so caught up in doing the work of ministry until we forget the God of the work. At one point in my life, I found myself participating in a whole lot of God related activities, but if the truth be told I could not relate to God. He was not my focus, guide or my head.

When the year of 1999 came in it was designated as the year of supernatural birthing (the number 9 = birthing). It seemed like everywhere I turned ministers were instructing people to "push" for their spiritual promise was about to be birthed. Disapprovingly, the Spirit of the Lord spoke to me and said, "Some of them are not even pregnant; and even if they are, the baby is not even mine." We all know it takes sexual intercourse to produce a seed in the natural. As saints, we have an intimate relationship with God through our worship, or at least we should. However, when we aim our seeds of worship toward a vessel God didn't ordain, a bastard baby is produced. When we are intimate with everyone and everything but God, how can we expect to give birth to His promised seed? So I ask you, how many babies have you produced that God didn't father?

In September 1999, the Lord told me that I had miscarried too many of His babies and because those promises were birthed prematurely they died. Natural miscarriages occur because of genetic problems in the fetus, infection, hormonal imbalance and incompatibility between blood types (Bovo 84). Spiritual miscarriages can occur for many different reasons. First, the spiritual womb may not be strong enough to carry the weight of what God has called an individual to carry. The process of God prepares you to be able to handle whatever you must endure to carry God's promise. Another reason for spiritual miscarriages is found within the "fetus" itself. Naturally, the unborn child can contract a diseases, infection or develop a deformity. This can be a result of what the mother has exposed the child to and other times there maybe no medical explanation for this occurrence. It is imperative that we protect what God has placed in us by praying, fasting and consecrating; we must cover what God has placed in us.

When you talk about being pregnant with God's purpose, timing is everything. Our lives have been divinely orchestrated, from the conceiving of the promise through its development to its delivery. We must recognize that this is God's puppet show and He is the Puppet Master. We are mere puppets who must recognize that only He can pull the strings for us. I decided that I did not want to miscarry anymore of God's babies, neither did I want to give birth to any bastard babies (offspring not fathered by God). What we must realize is that babies in the natural are carried for nine months. Nevertheless, there have been instances where babies were overdue and carried beyond the normal time frame. In addition, some babies are also born prematurely and survive, like myself! As you will learn later, God's timetable is nothing like our own. However, you can rest assure that if God fathered your baby, it will come into fruition at the appointed time.

How Long? Not Long! (Read Gen. 12-22)

There is no way we can discuss being pregnant with a seed of promise without discussing Abraham. From the first account we have in the Bible where God spoke to Abraham, his faith in God's word was being tested. In Genesis 12, God told Abram to leave his country, family and his father's house. All of these things represented what was familiar to Abram. Sometimes familiarity brings complacency. In these states, it is hard for God to complete His work in us. When God instructed me to move from Jacksonville Florida to Columbus Ohio to attend World Harvest Bible College, I was terrified! I did not want to move almost 1,000 miles away from what was familiar to me. At any rate, God showed me how the dependence I had on my mother, older sister and brother caused me to live independently from Him. It was because of this independence that the cords of attachment I had needed to be snipped away. God is not about to take a back seat to anyone.

We are espoused to jealous man! As a result of me placing God in His proper place, which is first in my life, my relationship with my family has grown stronger and deeper. It's all about obedience.

The fulfillment of Abram's promise depended solely on him being obedient to what God had spoken. God promised to make him a great nation, bless him, make his name great and said he (Abraham) would be a blessing to those who blessed him and those who cursed him would be cursed. Abram's blessing depended solely on his faith in God's word. Faith without works is dead and unless we put faith and trust together, faith alone is null and void. When we exhibit trust in God we show Him we have complete confidence in His ability. Even though we may not have a clue as to where we are going or how we are going to get there, we find comfort in knowing that God knows where we have been, where we are and where we are going. We must place our entire lives in His hands and allow Him to be God!

The Plight of Ishmael

Once God gave Abram his assignment and told him what the ultimate result would be, God did not immediately begin to fulfill His promise. Sometimes it is necessary for God to see where our heart is before we see the fulfillment of the vision that has been planted on the inside of us. One of the first actions God instructed Abram to take was to "get out of your country, from your family." In response, Abram departed from Ur with his wife Sarai and his nephew Lot, who was later removed from being with Abram, see Genesis 13.

After Abram's first act of obedience, God told him he would allow him to produce an heir from his own loins (see Gen. 14:4-5). In addition, his descendants would be compared to the stars in the heavens! Nevertheless, up to this point Abram hadn't disclosed to Sarai what God had promised them. It is so critical that we don't allow people to take our eyes off of what God has already said will be. Everyone will not believe in the promises of God concerning your life. That is why it is best not to share something's; keep them between you and God. Why, you ask? Let's see what happened to Abraham.

Abram allowed Sarai to persuade him into having "relations" with the maidservant Hagar. As a result, Hagar conceived and bore a son named Ishmael. It was not until after Ishmael was born that Abram and Sarai realized they had handled matters out of their flesh. Though Ishmael was a mistake, he could not be thrown away or forgotten. God will take our mistakes and make them work out for our good. I want you to think about something for a moment. Think about all the Ishmael's you have produced out of the works of your flesh. The ones you thought you were not going to make it through; the ones you thought were going to take the very life from you. Guess what? You made it! The devil thought he had you, but you got away! God will take those things we give birth to through illegitimate means and still bless them, as He did Ishmael (see Gen. 17:20).

Experiencing A Name Change

Abram was seventy-five years old when God first spoke to him about moving from his place of familiarity to a place God would later reveal to him. However, Abram was 100 before he saw the fulfillment of the promised seed. That lets me know God sometimes will make us wait for the fulfillment of our promises also. If God were to give us everything we asked for when we ask for it, how would we react? If we would be honest with ourselves, we know we would not be prepared for those things. God provides for us a time of preparation, from the time of conception to delivery. I have never seen a baby born in the embryonic stage and survive. The same holds true for the delivery of the spiritual promise. If we want our babies to "come out" alive and kicking, we must wait for them to develop properly and fully.

Before the birth of the promised seed, change had to take place in both Abram and Sarai. They could no longer be identified by their old names, for they were about to see in the natural what

God had shown them in the spirit for years. Therefore, God changed their names to fit who their destiny's had commanded them to become. Instead of Abram, which means "high father", he would now be known as Abraham, "father of a multitude" (Nelson 13-15). And no longer would his wife be Sarai or "my (Abram's) princess", but Sarah, meaning "princess of nation" (Nelson 590). They were destined to become not only the mother and father of a few, but of a nation. Now that Abraham and Sarah had been adequately prepared, the time had finally come to receive their child of promise.

The Promised Seed

God is so awesome! He could have allowed Sarah to become pregnant at any time during her childbearing years. But He wanted to wait until she was in a barren situation. Only God will tell you that you will bare fruit out of season. God does not want to share His glory with anyone. If He were to allow things to happen when we think they should, we may ignorantly give credit to another or ourselves. God waits until we are at the end of our rope and in a state of barren because man's extremity is God's opportunity.

Once the seed of promise is born, God may require us to sacrifice it. So I ask you, Is the fulfillment of your promise more important to you than your relationship with God? Before you say no, give it some serious thought. At some point, we may find we are motivated to stay with Him for what we can get instead of what we can give. Check your motives, only you know the real drive behind your pursuit for a mate, earthly possessions, etc. However, when your motives are pure, you will not give God's request for a sacrifice a second guess. In Genesis 22:5, Abraham declared to his servants, " . . . the lad and I will go worship, and we will come back to you." He proceeded to build an altar, bind Isaac and prepared to slay him. That was a true test of Abraham's faith in God's ability to provide a worthy sacrifice unto Himself. So even if God asks you to offer your promised seed unto Him for a sacrifice, though you may not see anything near the altar, I encourage you to look for the ram that will be caught in the thicket by its horns. God has a ram in the bush for you!

Divine Intimacy

> "As the deer pants for the water brooks,
> so pants my soul for you, O God" (Ps. 41:1).

When we are thirsty for God we acknowledge that nothing or no one else can quench our thirst. Any other means of fulfillment are cheap imitations and will only leave us longing once again. When we experience intimacy on a spiritual level, it is as if God is saying, "I want you in to me, see?" Do you not desire to know God the way He longs for you to? Wouldn't it be nice to walk in the spirit so much until it doesn't take you three hours of praise and two hours of worship before you hook into His presence? God wants this for us but the only way this will happen is by seeking God on an individual level. Now, I can't give you ten steps to seeking God; everyone's relationship is different. What I can tell you is this: You can't seek God at the movies, mall or hanging around a crowd. You find God by getting into His presence on a daily basis and by allowing Him to give you the steps to a more close net relationship with Him. All it takes is an earnest pursuit.

Food for Thought

One more thing about the seed: "I have been young and now am old, yet I have not seen the righteous forsaken, nor his descendants (seed) begging bread" (Ps. 37:25). When you think of the greatness of carrying God's seed of promise on the inside of you, fear may attempt to grip you. However, look at what this Scripture says. God will not allow anything He fathered to go lacking. Whatever seed He has planted within you, He will help you take care of it. So I ask you, what seed has God impregnated within you that is being developed as you read? Is it ministering, pastoring, writing a book, or being a physician? No matter what the promised seed on the inside of you is, if it's God's baby, He will finance, manage, guide and lead it!

Questions to Ponder

1. Do I know what my purpose in life is? If so, what is it?

_____

_____

_____

_____

_____

_____

2. Have I made any moves to fulfill what I believe God has instructed me to do? If yes, what steps have I taken? If no, why haven't I made any moves to walk in my destiny?

_____

_____

_____

_____

_____

3. What lesson(s) can I learn from Abraham and Sarah?

_____

_____

_____

_____

_____

Chapter Five

Write the Vision

"My heart is overflowing with a good
theme; I recite my composition
concerning the King; My tongue is the
pen of a ready writer" (Ps. 45:1).

Read Habakkuk 1-4

The Prophet Habakkuk, meaning embrace, is the eighth of the twelve minor prophets. Nothing is known about Habakkuk except for his name. The date the book of Habakkuk was written is an approximation, between 625 B.C. and 586 B.C. During this time, the balance of power was shifting from the Assyrians to the Babylonians. Assyria's domination came to an end with the destruction of its capital city of Ninevah by the invading Babylonians in 612 B.C (Nelson 1361). As a result, we find Habakkuk questioning God about how such wicked people were allowed to triumph over the righteous.

In chapter 1:1-5, Habakkuk asks God two questions: "How long shall I cry, and You will not hear?" and "Why do You show me iniquity and cause me to see trouble?" Habakkuk felt that "plundering and violence are before me", "the law is powerless" and "the wicked surround the righteous." God responds by saying, " . . . Be utterly astounded! For I will work a work in your days which you will not believe though it were told you." God explains He is raising up the Chaldeans to bring forth chastisement upon Judah, and to also bring them to where they needed to be in Him. Judah had fallen into moral and social decay with violence, oppression of the poor and corruption running rampant. Habakkuk doesn't seem to be satisfied with the responses God has given him, for while he understands Judah's need for correction, he does not feel the correction should come from such a wicked and perverse people (verses 12-17). Hebrews 12:6 reads, " . . . Whom the Lord loves He chastens, and scourages every son whom He receives." The way God chooses to discipline us is up to His discretion. Though we may feel His rod of correction is a bit too harsh, He only corrects us because He loves us. In addition, He only desires to get us to where we need to be in Him. Verse 12 declares God had appointed the Chaldeans for judgment and marked them for the correction of Judah.

"For the time has come for judgment to begin
at the house of God; and if it begins with us first,
what will be the end of those who do not obey the
gospel of God." (I Peter 4:17)

Judgment is not only used as an avenue of discipline and reproof, but also as a venue of development and spiritual maturation. God is not obligated to govern and chastise those who are not His. Whatever method God decides to use as correction will work for the good of those who love Him!

In verse 13, Habakkuk tells God, "You are of purer eyes than to behold evil, and cannot look on wickedness. Why do You look on those who deal treacherously, and hold Your tongue when the wicked devours a person more righteous than he?" Habakkuk agreed that the Judean people were wicked; but surely they were more righteous than the despicable Chaldeans! That reminds me of the "holier than thou" syndrome some of us in the Body of Christ suffer from. When we see someone who may have a problem with fornication or drugs, we want to degrade them and send them to hell in a hand basket. But you would rather hide the fact that you can't keep your tongue under control. Sin is sin! There is no way around it and no sin ranks higher than another. Isaiah 64:6 reads, "But we are all like an unclean thing, and all our righteousness are like filthy rags; we all fade as a leaf." In essence, a man's righteousness means nothing without a lifestyle that runs parallel.

In the beginning of chapter two, we find Habakkuk retreating to his watchtower to wait for God's response to his additional inquires. I believe the watchtower symbolizes Habakkuk's point of separation and isolation. Up to this point, he had been so focused on the circumstances at hand until deliverance seemed like an impossibility. It is imperative we allow God to set us apart from the busyness of our dilemmas and everyday situations. In order for us to understand what God is doing, our focus needs to be realigned from the impossibility of our situations to God's ability to work in us and on our situations simultaneously. Once Habakkuk positioned himself to hear from God, he is given these instructions:

> "Write the vision and make it plain upon the
> tablets, that he may run who reads it. For the
> vision is yet for an appointed time; But at the end
> it will speak and it will not lie. Though it tarries, wait
> for it; Because it will surely come, It will not tarry."

The word vision (chazon, Greek), means a revelation which comes through sight. In a vision, God enables a person to supernaturally see reality from a different realm while remaining in time and space. Habakkuk understood God's admonition clearly because He revealed matters to him by visible means. God's instructions to Habakkuk was for him to perceive the vision with his natural ear and then digest it into his spirit so that it may become food for his soul. Once he could hear and receive the vision, he could place action or give feet to what God had said. It was not enough to hear and believe what God had said; Habakkuk needed to add works to his faith. In addition, Habakkuk was to wait for the appointed time. To wait means to stay in a state of expectation and continue in patience. This means that even though the vision has not manifested into the natural realm, doubt and unbelief should not cause Habakkuk and Judah to loose sight of what God had said. The remainder of chapter two describes the events that will take place according to God's plan. Since God had decided to use a wicked people to bring judgment on His people, the wickedness of the Chaldeans was not going to be ignored. The same cup they had forced others to drink, they were going to be required to drink of also. "You are filled with shame instead of glory. You also—drink! And be exposed as uncircumcised!" (verse 16).

In chapter 3, Habakkuk realizes God's sovereignty: He can do whatever He wants to, however and whenever He decides to do it! Although Habakkuk did not agree with how God decided to bring judgment on His people, he realized that:

> "Though the fig tree may not blossom, nor fruit
> be on the vines; Though the labor of the olive may
> fail, and the fields yield no food; . . . Yet I will rejoice
> in the Lord, I will joy in the God of my salvation."
> (verses 17-18).

Sometimes the things we go through places so much weight and pressure upon us until will feel like it would be better if we just died. Have you ever been so burdened down until you could not get into God's presence? Have you ever felt as if everything you needed to say was embedded deep into your heart, but you found it difficult to make the transfer to your tongue to utter the words that were on the inside? Just know you are not the only person who has been to this place and you will not be the last! When you feel like God has left you, He is closer than you realize. When it seems as though you can't get into contact with God, become a God chaser. Do whatever you must to get His attention. Put that chicken leg down for a few days; don't answer the phone for a night. Sacrifice those things your flesh thinks it cannot survive without and allow your spirit to reign in dominion.

Psalm 91 reads, "He who dwells in the secret place of the Most High shall abide under the shadows of the Almighty." If you want to go where God is, you must find a "secret place". This simply means that if you want to abide under the protection of God, you must live in His presence. I know it is much easier said than done, for when you are burdened down the last thing your flesh wants to do is pray and get into God's presence. Can I enlighten you on a little something? The flesh delights in anything that goes against the promises of God. I know God has given me a vision for what He has called me to do. However, it seems like I am no closer to seeing this vision manifest into the natural than when He first showed it to me. If the truth were told, I am really struggling with something's I would prefer not to be dealing with right now. However, I realize that the anointing comes with a price, and it does not exempt me from struggles but qualifies me! Let me also interject this. My battle is not a result of anything worldly or fleshly. When you are serious about doing those things that God has called you to do, and you refuse to allow the desires of the flesh to dictate your actions, hell becomes infuriated! My flesh would love to give up and say this is too much for me to handle. In actuality, it is too much for Ivy alone to handle. But thanks be to God that Ivy is not alone! Even though I may feel like I am by myself at times, I am not. As you will find out later, when God separates you from things and people, He places you into a position where you can't hear anyone else but Him. So what, your phone isn't ringing and no one is asking you to go to the movies or out to eat. God is just doing some major construction work in and on you. I admonish you to let the master Builder restore your current temple!

Habakkuk found great difficulty being named the visionary of God's plan of using the Chaldeans to bring forth judgment to the people of Judah. Since Judah was considered to be God's chosen people, they had the tendency to believe they were beyond reproach. This attitude of exemption caused them to receive a stricter judgment because " . . . the Lord has chosen Jacob (the father of Judah) for Himself," (Ps. 135:4). Habakkuk discovered that being among God's elect yields great responsibility, as well as some awesome benefits. Through this entire occurrence, he learned one important principle: "In everything give thanks, for this is the will of God in Christ Jesus concerning you," (1 Thess. 5:18). Whether he understood or not, Habakkuk realized God was doing what was best for his people; he just was a visionary of the process.

Food for Thought

"Where there is no revelation or prophetic vision
the people cast off restraint; But happy is he
who keeps the law," (Proverbs 29:18).

A vision is nothing more than a divine strategy given to us by God to guide us into whatever He has for us. The vision of God insures us that we will reach our optimal level of greatness in Him. God can and will give you a vision for your ministry, home, marriage, family, business and everything else that concerns you. Unfortunately, you will find that many people will become excited about the thought of a fulfilled or manifested vision, but not many people want to do the leg work required to bring the vision to pass. Fore instance, I just completed my first singles/young adult conference. Trust me, nine months ago, EVERYONE was excited about the conference and wanted to offer assistance. However, as time drew closer and finances became scarce, the manpower also became non-existent. But thanks be to God for the many rams in my bush. God will always have the people we need at the time we need them to birth His vision through. With that said, I encourage you to keep your eye on the one who gave you the vision and not the vision itself. The magnitude of what God has spoken will always seem larger than what we can handle.

Nevertheless, I guarantee that if God gave the vision, it is He who is responsible for the manifestation. All you need to do is step back and watch Him move!

Questions to Ponder

1. Has God given me a vision concerning my future endeavors? If so, what is it?

_____

_____

_____

_____

_____

_____

2. When my natural position is contrary to what God has shown me in the spirit, how do I deal with it?

_____

_____

_____

_____

_____

_____

3. What lessons can I learn from the prophet Habakkuk and his dealings with the people of Judah?

_____

_____

_____

_____

_____

_____

Chapter Six

A Spiritual Ear Infection

"He who has an ear, let him hear
what the Spirit says to the churches,"
(Rev. 3:22).

In the Scripture referenced above, John specifically speaks to those who have an ear to hear the voice of God and not to those who just have a pair of ears. In order for a person to hear God's voice with assurance and clarity, he or she must be submitted to His will, committed to His way and purged of all the desires of the flesh. But, what happens when a person is doing all they know how to do and yet they have trouble distinguishing the instructions of God when He speaks? How can one be sure that it is God's voice you are hearing and not that of the adversary or the will of your own flesh? Take a look at this.

About two years ago I came down with an ear infection. Though I can remember having one as a child, there was something about this pain that was different. Initially, it began as a slight headache. As a result, I took a few pills and figured it would be all right the next morning. Little did I know I was only treating a symptom and not the problem. The next day I was awaken to a pain in my right ear that was unbearable. The slightest touch or noise drove me to tears and unpleasant facial expressions. I pressed my way to class that day and eventually went chapel service. I ultimately had to move my seat in chapel service because the sounds that erupted from the speakers were too much for my ear. The cotton I had placed in my ear did not block anything. For the next couple of days my ear was sensitive to the slightest touch or sound. I didn't want to hear anything and I definitely didn't want anyone touching my ear! Because I didn't have medical insurance at the time, I had to turn to home remedies and prayer, of course! (I would've prayed even if I had medical insurance, let me make that clear!) Even though my ear is now healed, I will never forget that experience for the rest of my life.

It amazes me how God can use the natural things in our lives to show us things in the spirit. God allowed me to see how my physical impairment had a spiritual connotation. There are many people in the Body of Christ who are suffering from a spiritual ear infection. Just as a natural ear infection impairs one's ability to function as usual, a spiritual ear infection does the exact same thing. When you are unable to hear God like you maybe accustomed to, your entire world is in a frenzy, or a least it should be!

According to Webster, the ear is the organ of hearing. Another definition says having an ear means that one is able to distinguish musical sounds, to heed or regard. An infection is the process of tainting with disease or the communication of bad qualities. With these two definitions in mind, we can conclude when one suffers from an ear infection the ability to hear and distinguish certain sounds is tainted by disease.

When God speaks to us, His voice is always clear and concise. God does not speak through a muzzle nor does He speak with a stutter. What may not be clear however, is our ability to receive what He says. Some of us say we can't hear God clear when that is really not the issue. The issue is that He maybe saying something which makes us uncomfortable and may cause us to come out of our areas of solace. If you feed your spiritual man constantly by praying, fasting, consecrating, living a life of praise and worship and going to church, there is no reason why you should have a problem with hearing God. When you feed your spiritual man properly, being able to distinguish between God and the devil will be second nature. The devil will always speak what is contrary to what God has told you by directly speaking to you or through His Word. If you hear a voice telling you to move quickly on something and you know you have already heard the Lord say "Wait", don't be fooled. Remember, the enemy is quite smooth and conniving.

Now, when you don't feed your spirit you allow the ways of the world to cloud your ability to hear God's voice. Also, when you consult everyone but God, you run the risk of their voice becoming louder than His voice. If you set yourself in a position to hear, I guarantee you, His voice is quite clear. Your relationship with God can be so airtight until His voice will be as clear as someone who is sitting next to you. What we must do is get rid of all the disease carrying elements in our lives.

Questions to Ponder

1. Have I ever been stricken with a "spiritual ear infection"? Explain.

_____

_____

_____

_____

_____

2. Do I have a problem distinguishing between God's voice and that of the enemy? If yes, what measures can I take to be able to detect the difference?

_____

_____

_____

_____

_____

PART II

Sanctified

A Stepping Stone

No emotion can be compared to the joy that God supplies,
This unconditional feeling can cover every area of our
lives.
But sometimes we face situations that we don't
understand,
And somehow they cause us to question our spiritual
man.

Even when things look gray, the Bible declares all things
will work out for the best,
Because in God we are more than conquerors and can
withstand any test.
So don't be perplexed, for God has not left you alone,
Though the devil set your trials up to be a stumbling
block, God is using them as A Stepping Stone.

Stumbling blocks are designed to lead the people of
God into sin,
For the devil knows his time is short, for he has a
predetermined end.
God never said we would not have storms, He just
provides us with the umbrella for the rain,
He also promised us His perfect peace that would
somehow ease the pain.

God uses stepping-stones to move us into a higher
spiritual place,
And in the meantime, He covers us with His unmerited
favor, also known as grace.
So, I admonish you to use your situations as stepping-
stones,
For God is about to show out in your life, are you ready
for the unknown?

Chapter Seven

Old Fashion Holiness

"Now may the God of peace Himself
sanctify you completely; and may your
whole spirit, soul and body be preserved
blameless at the coming of our Lord
Jesus Christ," (I Thess. 5:23).

Sanctification . . . Purification . . . Holiness . . . These words
have become obsolete in the Body of Christ. And why do I make
that statement? I'm glad you asked. It is because the Church as
a whole would prefer not to be identified as being holy or
sanctified. There was a time when people of God took pride in
being called a "holy roller" or "sanctified Susie". But today, we
would prefer to be "known" and popular. We as a whole, are
comfortable with doing just enough to make it into heaven, but
not enough to be identified as the peculiar and chosen generation
God has called us to be, see I Peter 2:9.

Holiness is defiantly not a look. You cannot wear pants,
make up, short sleeves and use only natural herbs in your
hair, but we know these attributes only denote a stereotype
and not a lifestyle. I can remember when I first received the
call into ministry and being instructed by my pastor to meet
with the missionary board. While at this training session, three
ladies and myself were told what was expected of us as aspiring

69

missionaries. Well in actuality, we were given a list of no's: No pants, No makeup, No jewelry while preaching, No open toe shoes at church, No colored nail polish, No coming to church without socks or hosiery, etc. No one bothered to warn us about the level of spiritual warfare you experience once you begin to walk in your God-ordained call. No one gave us pointers on how to study the Bible or suggested study material. We were just told we had to look holy! And you know, I'm not pointing fingers at anyone for anything, because I am sure they were only teaching us what they were taught.

No wonder the Church is in its current state; our view of holiness is misguided. If we only teach people how to dress the outward man to fulfill the obligations of a persona, then the inward man is destined to be filled with dead man's bones. We, as a Body have learned what holiness is not, but no one has taken the time to teach us what holiness is. God works from the inside out, not the outside in. When we learn the true meaning of sanctification, the outer man can and will not remain unchanged.

Before we go any further, let's look at a few definitions, according to Webster, of course:

1. Sanctification: the process of making holy; to hollow; to make pure from sin.
2. Purification: the process of making pure or clear; to free from admixture; to free from guilt.
3. Holy: to be free from sin.
4. Consecration: the process of being set aside for sacred uses; to dedicate to God.

We have already learned that salvation involves man being redeemed from sin. However, Jesus did not die a malicious death just so we could be saved.

"For He Himself is our peace, who has
made both one, and has broken down the

middle wall of separation, having abolished
in His flesh the enmity, that is, the law of
commandments contained in ordinances,
so as to create in Himself one new man
from the two, thus making peace, and that
He might reconcile them both to God in one
body through the cross, thereby putting to
death the enmity," (Eph. 2:14-6).

Jesus' main purpose for coming to Earth and dying the death of the cross was so that man could be reconciled back to God. From the beginning of time, God designed man to have close fellowship with Him in a personal relationship. However, when man sinned in the Garden of Eden, the act of sin placed opposition or enmity between God and humanity (read Gen. 3:1-5). Even though we must face certain consequences for our sinful actions, God will never leave us without hope. When Satan planted the seed of discord within Adam and Eve, he thought it would prohibit the birth of the seed that would bruise his head. What we must realize is Satan is not after our material possessions; he is after our ability to reproduce greatness. If he can plant a seed of destruction to get us off our focus and keep us from fulfilling our destiny, then he will do it. We cannot be ignorant of his devices. We must recognize him for the conniving antagonist he is!

When looking at the definitions for sanctification, we see the process involves making one pure and holy. Consider this parallel. When you are preparing to make a cake from scratch, you first gather all of the necessary ingredients, e.g. flour, sugar, butter, milk, vanilla or lemon extract, eggs, etc. However, when you put these ingredients together, what you have is batter, not a cake. In order for the cake to be made, it must be baked for a set time and then tested to make sure it has cooked thoroughly. If the cake is cut before it has cooled, it may crumble before it reaches the serving dish. Though it may have been done, enough time had not elapsed to ensure its consistency!

The process of sanctification is quite similar to this. When God redeemed us from sin, that was only the first day of the rest of our lives. Being sanctified consists of a whole lot of ingredients that the Holy Spirit will instruct us on how they go together. Notice that one of the definitions for purification is "to free from admixture". When we come to God fresh out of the world, there are a lot of things in us that need to be taken out before God can start building a firm foundation in us. We have to be cleansed from old ways of doing things, purged from past lifestyles, healed from hurts and so forth. Being made holy is not a one-time thing. Every morning we wake up and make a conscious decision to dedicate our lives to the Lord, we are being made holy. Even if we sin, when we choose to repent, we are being made holy.

> "I beseech you therefore, bretheren, by the mercies of God, that you present your bodies a living sacrifice, holy, acceptable to God, which is your reasonable service," (Rom. 12:1).

Consecration involves allowing yourself to be set-aside for a holy purpose. As you read in Chapter five, Habakkuk retreated to his watchtower, away from the people so he could hear God clearly. When we consecrate ourselves before God, we dedicate our total being to Him. It is as if we don't take our next breath unless God gives the O.K. I know that may be just a little exaggerated, but when you desire God to be first and foremost in your life, you will go through desperate measures to obtain the intimate fellowship your spirit man yearns for. You must decide within yourself what your answer to this question is: How bad do I really want God to be priority in my life?

Food for Thought

From the time we ask God to save us until we take our last breath, we are being made holy. While we are being made holy,

God purifies us and cleanses us so there will be no traces of the world's residue on or in us. Only then are we considered to be sanctified and able to consecrate ourselves before God.

Questions to Ponder

1. What false ideals about sanctification, purification and holiness have I been taught?

_____

_____

_____

_____

_____

_____

2. Have these ideals had a negative affect on my making the decision to live saved? Explain.

_____

_____

_____

_____

_____

_____

3. As an individual, what steps can I take to live a consecrated life before God?

_____

_____

_____

_____

_____

_____

Chapter Eight

Becoming Weightless

"Come unto Me, all you who labor and
heavy laden, and I will give you rest,"
(Matt. 11:28).

The world is obsessed with fitness and getting rid of those
extra, unwanted, love handles. From counting calories, to fact
grams and watching one's cholesterol, American has done well
to stress the importance of keeping in shape. Now, don't
misunderstand me. As people of God we ought to be concerned
with how we maintain our earthly vessels. We cannot expect to
effectively fulfill our purpose being out of shape and diseased
stricken in our bodies. The Bible refers to the body as being the
temple of the Holy Ghost, therefore, we do not belong to ourselves.
For this very reason, God must be glorified not only in our spirit,
but also in our mortal bodies (read I Cor. 6:19). So people of
God, take care of you body!

"Therefore we also, since we are surrounded
by so great a cloud of witnesses, let us lay
aside every weight, and the sin which so
easily ensnares us, and let us run with
endurance the race that is set before us,
looking unto Jesus the author and finisher

of our faith, who for the joy that was set before
Him endured the cross, despising the shame,
and has set down at the right hand of the throne
of God," (Heb. 12:1-2).

Weight is defined as "a heaviness, pressure or a burden".
Now, think of a "weight" you are carrying right now. Before you
allow your mind to analyze your situation, tap into your spirit. A
weight is not necessarily a bad thing. Maybe you are carrying
the burden of having an unsaved loved one. Maybe you are
experiencing some things in your body. Maybe you are carrying
the weight of an old relationship because you are finding it difficult
to severe that soul tie. Whatever thing you are carrying, ask
yourself, "Could this be the reason why I feel like I cannot progress
toward my destiny in God?" If you are not ready to be honest
with yourself, ask the Holy Spirit to reveal it to you. Then open
your spirit to whatever He has to say.

If you have ever watched a track meet, you have probably
noticed that the participants do not run with barbells in their
hands. Neither do the women run in high heels or the men in
dress shoes. They are dressed in attire that corresponds with the
activity they are participating in. Likewise, if we are to run this
Christian race with endurance, we cannot carry the weights of the
world on our shoulders. If we continue to carry things that place
pressure on us and weigh us down, those things can become sin.
We know sin places a blockage in the line of communication
between God and His people. Weights produce distractions that
take our minds off of the things we are to be focused on. So take
those weights and cast them upon Jesus; He is the burden bearer!
If we expect to effectively run this race, we must be loosed from
these weights and place our spiritual eyes on the author and finisher
of our faith. A runner cannot run looking back at the opponents
who may be hot on his/her trail. This action may cause the runner
to become more concerned with who is behind him/her, and cost
them the race. Weights take our focus off of God and what He has
intended and places it on what the "eyes of the flesh" sees.

If you want to be free from the issues of heaviness which are present in your life, you must first realize you do have some weights and confess them. Next, ask the Holy Ghost to show you how to be loosed from the heavyweights in your life. As I said before, I don't believe in giving people a five-step program to the issues concerning their lives. What has worked for me, may not do a thing for you. The Bible tells us that the Holy Ghost is our teacher (John 14:26). We must make a demand on the Spirit of God which dwells on the inside of us and take responsibility for our individual relationships with God.

Questions to Ponder

1. What are the situations in my life which present themselves as weights in my relationship with the Lord? List them below.

_____

_____

_____

_____

_____

_____

2. Do I feel like the weights in my life have prohibited me from reaching my potential in God? How?

_____

_____

_____

_____

_____

_____

3. What steps am I willing to take to be loosed from the "weighty" matters in my life?

_____

_____

_____

_____

_____

_____

Chapter Nine

Spiritual Warfare

"For the weapons of our warfare are not
carnal but mighty in God for pulling down
strongholds," (II Cor. 10:4).

We are currently living in the time when all of the Bible prophecies we have so diligently read about are coming into reality. So-called men and women of God are not practicing the messages they are preaching in their lifestyles. Wolves are disguising themselves as sheep who come to ravish the flock of God. The Church at large contains the presence of those who have itching ears and refuse to endure sound doctrine and are yearning for the sugar coated, watered down version of the Bible. The devil is indeed busy; his actions should only make us as men and women of God busier. He knows his time is short, so he continues to walk about like a roaring lion, seeking whom ever he may devour. It seems as though the devil is more prepared than the saints of God are:

"Even the stork in the heavens knows
her appointed times; And the turtledove
the swift and the swallow observe the
time of their coming. But my people do
not know the judgment of the Lord," (Jer. 8:7).

If we expect to fight the enemy head on and be victorious in the battle, we must leave the elementary principles behind and move on into perfection. The adversary is not intimidated by anyone who is still trying to fight in the carnal realm. In other words, if you are still having problems keeping your dress down and pants up, spiritual warfare will sift you as wheat. If you are still bound by lust, alcohol, drugs, etc., ask God for deliverance first, walk in that deliverance and then come back to this chapter. Spiritual warfare is not a subject to be taken lightly! Don't get me wrong; I am not giving the devil more power than what he has. However, I want you to realize he does have some power, and as a result we must not be ignorant of his devices.

In this chapter, we will look into spiritual warfare and what it involves. Next, we will look at the whole armor of God by defining each part and then study how they work together. Lastly, we will look at the importance of prayer and how it relates to spiritual warfare. So I ask you, are you ready to get dressed?

What Are We Fighting For?

The main thing I want you to get out of this chapter is this: Spiritual warfare is a spiritual fight! That may seem quite elementary, but to be honest with you I think we tend to forget that. What we must remember is Satan is a spirit who must have a body to operate in. So, your enemy is not your supervisor, co-worker or an ex-boyfriend who won't take no for answer. It is the spirit at work on the inside of these individuals that is at war with the spirit of God on the inside of you.

Read Ephesians 6:10-20

About four years ago, I woke up in the middle of the night to use the restroom. As I stood by my bed, I realized I could not walk on my right foot I hopped to the bathroom not giving it a second thought; I just figured it would be all right in the morning.

Nevertheless, when I woke up the next morning to attend Sunday service, my foot was swollen and I could not put much pressure on it. I called a friend to drive me to church and had a nurse to look at it after service was over. She suggested that I go to the emergency room. I went later on that evening and the doctor on duty told me I was going to be treated for gangrene. I was given several prescriptions to begin taking immediately. Once I began to take the medications, within a 24-hour period, my condition became worse. The swelling went from my foot, to my ankle and up my leg. My foot and leg was twice its original size. I must admit, I was frightened! The devil began to say, "You're going to die!" My mother and sister drove two and a half hours to pick me up from school so that I could see my regular doctor. By this time, the swelling had gone down immensely. My doctor ran a series of tests and could not find anything; not even a trace of gangrene.

After this ordeal was over, I wanted to know what this was all about. I knew my foot and leg would not have swollen for any apparent reason. I began to pray and ask God for some answers to this puzzling situation. As a result, God did not answer me for about two weeks or so. I was praying, reading my Word, fasting and doing everything I knew to do to place myself into a position to hear from God. He still did not answer. I realize now that God sometimes wants to see how persistent we will be to get an answer from Him. Silence doesn't mean that God is ignoring us; sometimes our patience and persistence have to be tested. In essence, when you feel like you are down to nothing, God is up to something. You are closer to your answer than what you may think!

One day while at work, the Holy Spirit finally spoke to me and instructed me to read Ephesians 6:10-20. At this point, I hadn't heard from God for about two weeks. As I started to read about the whole armor, I said to myself, "I have this on; I think I have this on." Just then, I heard a small still voice say, "I didn't call you to think!" God then began to reveal to me that the enemy was trying to attack my health. I had just preached my first message two months earlier and the enemy was angry! As I mentioned before, he is after our ability to reproduce greatness. Whenever you make the decision to walk in your divine purpose, you are making strides towards God impregnating you with His seed of promise.

From that point until now, God has been teaching me about spiritual warfare. The devil doesn't have any new tricks, just revised strategies. That is why we must make sure our armor is on tight so no matter what way he decides to come, we will not be caught off guard. When we get so accustomed to him attacking us in certain areas, we have no problem recognizing him. However, as soon as he comes to us differently, we panic because he is trodding upon territory that is unfamiliar. It is imperative that we make sure our armor is not only on, but also secured and properly placed.

Strapped for the Struggle!

Paul realized the Church was up against a real enemy, who has power and is capable of defeating those who are not strong enough to endure his well thought out plans.

> "You therefore must endure hardship as
> a good soldier of Jesus Christ. No one
> engaged in warfare entangles himself
> with the affairs of this life, that he may
> please him who enlisted him as a
> soldier," (II Tim. 2:3-4).

When a person enlists into the armed forces, he or she must never lose sight of their purpose. As a soldier, an individual is being trained and equipped for future battle, when necessary. In comparison, as a soldier in the army of the Lord, we are also being prepared for future battle. The best time to prepare for war is not on the battlefield; that is where you put what you have learned into practice. You prepare for battle when things are tranquil and there are no bombs or grenades being fired.

Why fight?

Verse 12: "We do not wrestle against flesh and blood, but against-

1. Principalities/Powers: opposing forces of God.
2. The rulers of the darkness of this age: the place where evil reveals itself; these evil forces are superhuman, but are not all-powerful (Nelson 1783).
3. Spiritual host of wickedness in the heavenly places.

It would be so much easier if our enemy was of the flesh, then we could use carnal methods to defeat him. Since this is a spiritual fight, we have to rely on our spiritual man and equip ourselves with the weapons of the spirit to be adequately prepared.

What's the Attire?

Verse 13: "Therefore take up the whole armor of God, that you may be able to withstand in the evil day, and having done all, to stand."

The attire is the whole armor of God. This means we cannot pick and choose the parts we want to wear. It's all or nothing! I took a class on spiritual warfare and in this class I learned that Paul compared the armor of the Roman soldier to the armor of the believer. The following are notes I took from this class.

Verse 14: "Stand therefore, having girded your waist with truth, having put on the breastplate of righteousness,"

> **Loin Belt of Truth:** the loin belt was the least impressive part of the armor. However, it was the most important part because it held the other pieces of the armor together.

In addition, it was placed on first. It was not elaborate. The loin belt of truth represents the Word of God, in its written form, known as Logos. If you ignore the Word, you are purposefully allowing your armor to fall by the waste side. When a soldier of the Lord is in need of a word, he or she will reach for their Logos. The Word can and will make us complete, proficient, well fitted and thoroughly equipped for every good work. The loin belt also covered the soldier's reproductive organs. If the soldier was not protected in this area with the loin belt, he would have become sterile. Likewise, when we are strapped with the Word of God, the devil cannot destroy our ability to produce greatness. The Word of God protects our spiritual reproductive parts so that when we are intimate in worship, conception will not be a struggle or an impossibility.

Breastplate of Righteousness: the breastplate was made of bronze and/or brass. It began at the neck and ended at the top of the legs. Our righteousness is a result of the blood, see II Corinthians 5:21. It is easy for the enemy to attack for no reason and have us convinced that God will do things for everyone else but us The breastplate of righteousness protects us from the blows of the enemy; it cleanses us from the sense of unrighteousness and delivers us from condemnation. If the enemy can have us convinced that we are not going to make it to fulfill our destiny, we will not. It is not what we are which holds us back, it is what we think we are not. The breastplate was sculptured to make a person look muscular; what was underneath was hidden so that the opponent did not know what the physical stature of the person was behind the armor. When we have righteousness on securely, who we use to be and what we use to do is none of the devil's business! Righteousness places us in right standing with God, in spite of what our past lives may dictate.

Verse 15: "and having shod your feet with the preparation of the gospel of peace;"

The **Shoes** of the Roman soldier were made of brass. The first part was called "the grieve" and went from above the knee to the ankle. The second part of it went under the foot with 1-3 inch spikes on the bottom of the foot. These spikes were able to dig deep into the ground. To shod means to bind something tightly. Peace should be bound tightly so that it will not easily be removed in the time of confrontation. This Scripture conveys the type of peace which prevails or conquers. Preparation in the Greek gives the idea of a solid foundation. Colossians 3:15, states we should allow peace to "rule in our hearts." The word 'rule' as used in this sentence portrays an umpire or referee who judged athletic games in the ancient world. In essence, once we allow the peace of God to take residence in our heart, it will rule our lives.

Verse 17: "above all, taking the shield of faith with which you will be able to quench all the fiery darts of the wicked one."

Shield of Faith: there were different types of shields used in ancient times. The smallest shield was used for public ceremonies. The one used for battle was a door-sized shield which covered the entire man. It was made of woven layers of animal hide. It was as stern as steel, but was actually leather and had to be maintained. Maintenance was done everyday with a vile of oil. The shield was also submerged in water. If the shield was not taken care of, it could cost the soldier his life. The shield was saturated with oil to counteract the possibility of an arrow exploding upon impact. The oil represents the anointing. During biblical times, oil was used as a medical healing agent which was rubbed on soar muscles. In contrast, when God's hand is on a person, He is rubbing the presence of the Holy Spirit on them. Bless God! In addition, there were several types of fiery darts. The basic arrow was used with a bow. Another arrow was dipped in tar, set on fire and then dispatched. However, the arrow the fiery darts refer to is an arrow containing combustible fluids that would burst upon impact. However, if your shield has been submerged in the water of the Word and rubbed in the anointing, no fiery dart the enemy has will be able to penetrate your faith. Hallelujah!

Verse 17: "And take the helmet of salvation, and the sword of the spirit, which is the word of God."

Helmet of Salvation: was made of bronze and specific pieces covered the cheeks and jawbone to fit these areas tightly. Inside was a spongy-like material to protect the soldier from a possible blow from the enemy. Very long feathers were placed at the top of the helmet. Some helmets were shaped as animals. These headpieces were very beautiful to look at. Our salvation is beautiful. When we are tightly secured in our salvation, people will notice. When the helmet is not on, the enemy has an easy shot at the elements which support our salvation. The helmet protects the head, which conceals the mind. II Corinthians 10:4-5, tells us our spiritual weapons are to be used to pull down strong holds. In addition, this Scripture tells us that we should cast down the imaginations that attempt to be exalted against the knowledge of God. Stronghold means fortress, protection or prison. Strongholds do not go up overnight; they form over a period of time. They help construct walls to keep people out to guard against hurt; unfortunately, they also keep the Lord from healing an individual. To demolish or overthrow strongholds, we must recognize our responsibility in building them. Our minds need to be renewed or renovated. Imagination refers to a mind which has been trained to think logically. However, a mind which has been trained to think this way will have a problem with faith. We control our thought patterns. In addition, this Scripture admonishes us to bring our thoughts into captivity. Taking captive refers to a person who has been taken into custody with a spear to their backs. It connotes taking someone into a subordinate position and making them listen. We can make our thoughts sit in a subordinate position and submit to whatever the Word of God says.

Sword of the Spirit: This was the most expensive weapon. It was 19 inches and razor sharp on both sides of the blade. The tip of the sword was turned upward and the soldier would twist the sword inside the opponent before he pulled the sword out. It was a weapon of murder. The armor of God has given us has the ability to shred the enemy. This is when the written word or 'Logos' becomes the spoken word or "Rhema". A Rhema word is spoken clearly and in unmistakable terms. Rhema is a specific word the Holy Spirit quickens in your heart and mind at a specific time for a specific purpose. Rhema is when the Word comes alive and real to you. It is important to remember that you cannot have a Rhema word if Logos does not exist.

Verse 18: Praying always with all prayer and supplication for all the saints."

The Roman soldier's armor consisted of seven pieces. The one weapon Paul did not describe was the lance, better know as the javelin. The soldier did not wait for the enemy to come into his camp. The lance was thrown before the enemy entered into his territory. Even though prayer was the last spiritual weapon mentioned, it should be in operation constantly and consistently. At every possible chance, the **Lance of Prayer** should be disclosed before a spiritual attack comes.

Prayer: How to Get the Eyes and Heart of God

To make it simple, prayer is our way of communicating with God. Communication indicates a dialogue, not a monologue. Prayer doesn't consist of us giving God our 'must needs list'. When you pray, you talk to God and then allow him to speak to you. Most of the time we end our prayers without giving God the opportunity to respond.

King Solomon, the son of David had been chosen to build God's house, see I Chronicles 17:11-12 and 28:9-21. Once Solomon finished the temple, he dedicated it back to God. In Solomon's prayer of dedication in II Chronicles 6, he wanted to know the purpose of God's request for this temple. In response, God told Solomon he had chosen this place for Himself as a house of sacrifice, II Chronicles 7:12. The temple of God is a place designed by God for the people of God to hear from God.

Read II Chronicles 7:13-16

Sometimes in our daily walk we feel as though the heavens are shut up and our land is devoured. However, God designed the lance of prayer as the believer's weapon to get into contact with Him. If we have all the elements of verse 14 when we pray, God has no choice but to fulfill His Word.

> "God is not a man, that He should lie, nor
> a son of man that He should repent. Has
> He said, and will He not do? Or has He
> spoken, and will He not make it good?"
> (Num. 23:19)

"If my people who are called by my name
will humble themselves, and pray and seek
my face, and turn from their wicked ways,
then, I will hear from heaven, and will
forgive their sin and heal their land,"
(II Chron. 7:14).

Requirements to be Met:

1. **My people:** "But we are a chosen generation, a royal priesthood, a holy nation, His own special people, that you may proclaim the praises of Him who called you out of darkness into His marvelous light," (I Pet. 2:9).

There are a lot of people who are claiming to know and love God, who have never accepted Him as Savior. Being able to preach and teach does not qualify a person to be a part of God's chosen generation. Jesus said in Matthew 7:22-23 that many would boast about the works they did in His name; however, his response will be "I never knew you, depart from me." So in essence, make sure you're one of His.

2. **Called:** "Who has saved us and called us with a holy calling, not according to our works, but according to His own purpose and grace which was given to us in Christ Jesus before time began," (II Tim. 1:9).

According to Romans 8:30, God had His hand placed on you before the beginning of time. He knew the mistakes you would make and He still called you. God has summoned for you by name; now you must decide whether you will answer. While man will choose you because of whom you are, God calls you in spite of who you are. What an awesome God we serve!

3. **Humbled**: "Therefore humble yourselves under the
   mighty hand of God, that He may exalt you in due
   time," (I Pet. 5:6).

Proverbs 16:18 records, "Pride goes before destruction and
a haughty spirit before a fall. It is better to be of an humbled
spirit with the lowly than to divide the spoil with the proud. I
have seen people rely on sheer talent to preach, teach and sing.
The hearts of these individuals are full of pride because they
know they are talented so they feel their need for God is minimal.
At any rate, I love to see it when one who is not so talented takes
what they have and God places His anointing on them because
their heart is after pleasing Him only. This person will obtain
God's trust because their heart is pure.

4. **Pray**: "pray without ceasing," (II Thess. 5:17).
5. **Seek**: "First seek ye the Kingdom of God and His
   righteousness, and all these things shall be added
   to you," (Matt. 6:33).
6. **My face**: "When you said 'Seek my face,' my heart
   said to you, 'Your face, Lord, I will seek'," (Ps.
   27:8).

Seeking God's face is very important. Psalm 103:7 records
that God made His ways known to Moses and His acts to the
children of Israel. This is because Israel was only interested in
knowing God as a deliverer, but Moses desired to know Him as
Savior. We shortchange ourselves when we only pursue God for
what He can do and not who He is. Remember, the secret to
knowing God is wrapped up in discovering His personage, not
His actions.

7. **Turn**: "But if a wicked man turns from all his sins
   which he has committed, keeps all My statues, and
   does what is lawful and right, he shall surely live;
   he shall not die," (Ezek. 18:21).

To repent means to turn away from. I am afraid that most of what the Body of Christ does is apologize and call it repentance. Personally, I despise when someone says, "I'm sorry." I don't want anyone to be sorry; I want you to be sincerely remorseful for whatever took place. In addition, I want to know in my heart you will never do this again. "I'm sorry" just sounds appropriate for whatever the situation is; it does not necessarily hold a person to be accountable for what they have done. Likewise, God does not need our apologies. He desires for us to be convicted for the wrong we do and turn our backs on it forever, never to do it again.

God's ability to hear, forgive and heal is contingent upon us meeting the requirements listed before the word 'then'! Once all of His prerequisites are met, God promises to open His eyes and make His ears attend to our prayers, verse 15. To take it a step further, God will place His eyes and heart in the house He has chosen and sanctified. Since Jesus died on the cross and the veil in the temple has been torn, we are not obligated to enter into a specific temple to reach God. We have direct access to Him, through the Holy Ghost. I am getting a little excited about this, Glory! I realize that since I have been chosen of God and sanctified for His purpose, I carry His name on my body. For this reason, He gives me His eyes and His heart. I don't see things the same way and neither do I react to situations in my life the same way. I have been transformed into the sheer image of God!

Questions to Ponder

1. After reading this chapter, what is my understanding of spiritual warfare?

_____

_____

_____

_____

_____

_____

2. What parts of my armor could use a maintenance check?

_____

_____

_____

_____

_____

3. How can I increase the effectiveness of my prayers? Do I have all of the characteristics God requires of me as found in II Chronicles 7:14? Explain.

_____

_____

_____

_____

_____

Chapter Ten

The Process of Separation

"Come out from among them and be separate
says the Lord. Do not touch what is unclean,
and I will receive you," (II Cor. 6:17).

When a person makes the decision to follow God with their
whole heart, some things may be required of that individual.

"For you do not desire sacrifice or else I would
give it; you do not delight in burnt offering. The
sacrifices of God are a broken and a contrite
heart. These, O God, you will not despise,"
(Ps. 51:16-17).

The Old Testament ritual of animal sacrificing proved to
be a null and void form of worship. People performed their
duty of sacrificing a good or acceptable lamb, but their
lifestyles did not match their act of worship. A sacrifice does
not feel good; it brings you out of your area of comfort. God
does not want an outward form without the presence of a broken
spirit, a broken and a contrite heart. In this state you realize
your insufficiencies and God's abilities. We'll learn more about
becoming broken in chapter 15. Just remember, if it doesn't
hurt, it isn't a sacrifice.

When God calls you to be separated from something and/or someone, it is extremely difficult. As I stated before, my flesh did not want to separate from a man I love and place a relationship on hold in order for this book to be published. I could not effectively write about singleness when I was involved in a relationship. When you are focused on fulfilling the call of ministry that is placed upon your life, you will do all that is necessary to execute your destiny. This book has been in the works for many years. However, before now, I was trying to write solely from my ability and my experience. As a result, nothing was flowing. Now, I am writing as the Holy Ghost gives. The difference between then and now is that an anointing has been placed on my ability and my experiences.

What is Separation?

Separation is the act of setting apart for the purpose of sanctification. As we have already discovered, to sanctify means to make holy, to hollow and to make pure from sin. God wants each of His children to formulate an intimate relationship with Him and not just a casual acquaintance. When you detach yourself from things or people that may cause static or interference within the lines of communication between yourself and God, you allow Him to create a cavity or empty space in you. Becoming separated to the purpose of God demonstrates the willingness to submit to His will and dying to an individual agenda. It is in this empty place that we are driven to seek earnestly after God as the deer panteth for the water brook. This intense yearning cannot and will not be satisfied by anyone but God.

Separation leads to isolation, which means to place by one's self; to place in or as in an island, to insulate. Isolation is not just a physical state; it is also a spiritual position. The main idea is to detach your spirit from your thoughts (mind) and flesh (body). In turn, your spirit will become dominant and in control. Think of it this way. An island is a piece of land surrounded by water. John 4:14 references a fountain of water springing up into everlasting life. God sent Jesus to become that living water for us. It is through Him we obtain fulfillment of our deepest appentencies. Past methods are mediocre because we discover they are only short-term seasonal solutions.

The process of separation only last for a season, but its effects are everlasting. In addition, it maybe necessary for you to enter this process more than once, depending on where you are in your relationship with the Lord. Personally, in the past nine months God has required me to go into separation twice. Wait a minute. Something just registered in my spirit. I just realized the number nine means birthing in the spirit. Shammah! (God is here!) That means me being obedient and separating when God instructed me to directly effected this book being delivered out of my spirit. For the past nine months, I have been pregnant with this book. Everything I have been through during this time was critical to my baby's development. When I attempted to move ahead of God in my relationship with the man God has placed in my life, I was trying to make him the guardian of the promise God had fathered. This book is God's baby; He does not want any man taking the credit for something He fathered. When a woman is impregnated naturally it is done in private, behind closed doors. (At least, it is suppose to be!) Likewise, God does not impregnate us with His promise in a crowd. He waits for us to become separated and consecrated unto Him. You can't tell me that obedience is not better than sacrifice!

So what's stopping you? God could be trying to birth something through you and you want to be stubborn? Loose here! Just think each time you complete this process, the result will be this: A woman of God, full of fire who is led by the spirit and able to communicate it without restriction, restraint or reservation!

Food For Thought

Many people will never allow themselves to enter into a period of separation. Primarily, this process requires an individual to come face to face with who they are. Too often we find that many people do not like themselves and are afraid of being placed into a position where they would have to actually spend time alone. While in separation, there are no personal cheering sections to encourage you. There is no one to commend you on how well you can preach or how awesome of a worship leader you are. Separation demands that an individual examine their motives, lifestyle and every person and thing attached to them. Separation strips from you that which everyone else thought was God but in actuality it was only a residual presence of the anointing you should have had. No, there are no accolades or special privileges waiting on you in separation. Unfortunately, the Church has done well to ordain what God sees as profane! At any rate, I admonish you to take the step of faith and allow God to place you into this place. Yes, it is very lonely and painful, but at the same time very rewarding. You will find that being separated from people and things will bring you extremely close to God.

Questions to Ponder

1. What or who do I feel God is calling me to separate from?

_____

_____

_____

_____

_____

_____

2. What is hindering me from entering into this process?

_____

_____

_____

_____

_____

_____

3. How will separation help prepare me to give birth to what God has placed on the inside of me?

_____

_____

_____

_____

_____

_____

Chapter Eleven

God's Timetable

"For He says, 'In an acceptable time I have
heard you, and in the day of salvation
I have helped you," (II Corinthians 6:2).

In the previous chapter, we discussed separation and I told you how my separation led way to the delivery of this book into the natural. But what happens when God's timetable is a little longer than the natural birthing process of nine months? What happens when you have had an issue of blood for twelve years or you have been bent over for eighteen years?

"To everything there is a season, a time for every
purpose under heaven," (Eccl. 3:1).

While man's seasons change every three months, God may have you stay in one season for three days or the next three years. God's timetable is truly not the same as ours. Even when your spirit cannot trace His presence, you have to trust in His sovereign ability to be God in whatever place you're in.

"Kairos" Versus "Chronos"

The word for time or season has two Greek meanings in the noun tense. They are as follows:

1. Kairos: due measure, fitness proportion. A time suitable for a purpose. Kairos promotes the quality of time.
2. Chronos: a space of time, whether long or short; it implies duration. Chronos marks the quantity of time. (Vine 554)

Chronos is the span of time we are accustomed to. One of the first things you learn to do in grade school is place things in alphabetical (A-B-C) or chronological (1-2-3) order. So, when we are saved, we expect God to move the exact same way. However, what we fail to realize is while we live in Chronos, God operates in Kairos. He isn't concerned with our 1-2-3, A-B-C methods. For Him, B may come before A and 3 before 2. The way God operates for Wendy may not work for Evelyn. Nevertheless, if Evelyn waits for specific instructions from God, and not pattern herself after how God works for Wendy, she will save herself from a lot of extra disappointments. Whether you believe it or not, there is a blessing in waiting!

God is more focused on the quality of time, while man is consumed with time quantity. Just because an individual has been dealing with a particular situation for ten years does not mean they have learned what God intended. So many times we have to attend "summer school" in the spirit for certain issues in our lives because we didn't receive a passing grade during the initial "test". Regrettably, in God's school of trials and tribulations, we do not receive credit for length of time served. We must take the test of life and pass, taking with us those tools attained. In addition, it is not good enough for us to study, pass the test and forget the objectives the test exhibited. God may choose to issue a "pop quiz" later in life. So, as it reads in II Timothy 2:15: "Study to show thyself approved unto God, a workman that needeth not to be ashamed, rightly dividing the word of truth."

The Building of Another Temple

In Haggai 2:3-9, God told Zerubbabel to build a temple. However, after only a few weeks of work, progression stopped because the people began to compare it to the greatness of Solomon's temple. In their eyes, this temple was nothing. As a result, I am sure Zerubbabel became very discouraged. It is so important that we do not allow people to take us off of our focus. When God shows you a thing, your family and friends may not see it through the same set of spiritual eyes you have.

> " . . . Not by might nor by power, but by My
> spirit, says the Lord of host. Who are you,
> O great mountain? Before Zerubbabel you
> shall become a plain!" (Zech. 4:6-7a).

God had to remind Zerubbabel that it would be His spirit and not his [Zerubbabel's] ability that would complete the temple. Even though it had been seventeen years since the foundation had been lain, Zerubbabel could not become discouraged by the chronological time which had passed by. As mentioned before, the greatness of a building is no better than the foundation that supports it. The larger the building, the deeper you must dig in the ground. Before God can build us up, He must dig deep down into us to lay a solid foundation.

Food For Thought

Read Luke 2:41-52

There is something to be said about waiting for God's divine timing. God places us into certain realms in order to prepare us for what is to come. We may not understand His ways or His thoughts, but we must trust Him enough to know He knows just what He is doing. Though we may have His anointing on our lives and His ministry gift in us, He may place us in a position where we have to be subject to authority.

Like Jesus, we must learn to walk in obedience, for it was this position which allowed Him to have the favor of God and man. Man cannot curse what God has blessed; man may not like you, but he will reverence the presence of God in you.

Questions to Ponder

1. What season of my relationship with God am I currently in? What do I feel God is doing in me and through me at this time in my life?

_____

_____

_____

_____

_____

_____

2. Do I relate more to Kairos or Chronos? Why?

_____

_____

_____

_____

_____

_____

3. Have I allowed the opinions of others to take me off of the primary focus of fulfilling God's plan for my life? If yes, what can I do to change this?

_____

_____

_____

_____

_____

_____

Chapter Twelve

A Quick Work

"Be diligent to come to me quickly," (II Tim. 4:9).

I am sure a lot of you smiled a sigh of relief as you read the title of this chapter. I know, you've read so much about timing, seasons, waiting and building foundations until you are ready to hear about God doing something quick! Well, I hate to be the bearer of bad news, but I am sure this chapter is not about what many of you maybe thinking. I warn you now: This chapter is short, but explosive!

Read John 13:21-27

After Jesus had washed the feet of the disciples, He announced that one of them would betray Him. Surely, none of them could even fathom betraying the Messiah, they thought. They looked at each other with eyes of suspicion, trying to figure out who the culprit would be. One of the disciples, said to be John, asked who it would be. In response, Jesus said, "It is he to whom I shall give a piece of bread when I have dipped it." According to Jewish tradition, it was customary to dip a piece of bread and give it to a friend (Nelson 1604). Jesus gave the bread to Judas, who had already decided to betray Him as noted earlier in the chapter. At this point, Satan entered into Judas and possessed him. When Jesus saw this happening in the spiritual realm, He spoke to the spirit which had taken up residence on the inside of Judas and said, "What you do, do quickly." What Jesus was actually saying was this. I was born to die; I did not come to stay here. So devil, whatever you are going to do, do it. I have an appointment with destiny to meet; I have a seat on the right hand side of my Father to occupy. So whatever you do, do it quick!

> "That I may know him in the power of His resurrection and the fellowship of sharing in His sufferings, being conformed to His death," (Philippians 3:10).

For the most part, we as believers don't glory in the suffering aspect of our Christian walk. We want God's anointing on our lives and His approval on our ministries, however, we lack the tenacity it takes to go through life's test and trials. In the aforementioned Scripture text, Paul embraces the suffering aspect of his walk with God. Paul realized that every trail and tribulation he experienced were only being used as an avenue to bring him closer to the Christ he claimed he represented. If we are truly soldiers in the army of the Lord, then why are our lives as Christians minus the wounds and scars that are the tell signs that we've been in a battle? I know, if we all had our way we'd love for God to drop everything from heaven we need, when we needed it so we would never have to learn patience. We would be overwhelmed at the idea of never having to suffer any illnesses or go through any persecutions. However, if this were the case, would we ever come into the full knowledge of who God is?

The Amplified Bible says our sufferings allow us to become more deeply and intimately acquainted with God. For every struggle and bodily pain, there is a greater understanding of the wonders of God's purpose for us to obtain. Between the prophecy God has spoken over your life and the fulfillment or promise, there is a process. It is in the process that God reveals all those elements about us and in us that need to be stripped away from our lives. The process is the place where God peels off the layers of flesh, worldly ideals, personal agendas, self-driven motives and heals the hurts of the past to mold us into the person He desires us to become. The process is to grow you and prepare you for the things God has destined you to receive. The question is this: Are you ready to do what it takes to go through what you must to get to what God has promised you?

PART III

Satisfied

A Song in the Night

When I am in the middle of life's storms and the waves
are tossing to and fro,
I am in need of shelter from the winds and the rains, so
under your wings shall I go.
Your peace which surpasses all my understanding will
calm my every fear,
I place my complete trust in you, so to You I will draw
near.

You are a High Priest who can be touched with whatever
I am going through,
For in you I have power to speak to the mountain and it
will be removed.
Lord, in my darkest hour I need to know that You will
help me to fight,
That is why I find comfort in knowing, You will give me
"A Song in the Night".

A song in the night, a word of deliverance is what my
spirit yearns to hear,
The healing virtue from Your Word will wipe away all my
tears.
Lord, I thank You in advance for the things You are going
to do,
Because I realize that before I can recover all, I must be
able to pursue!

Chapter Thirteen

Lord, Play Me in Your Key

"Behold, You desire truth in the inward parts,
and in the hidden part You will make me
know wisdom," (Ps. 51:6).

According to Webster, to satisfy means to gratify fully, to content, to fulfill the claims of, to answer and to free from doubt. As a result, one could draw the conclusion that once a person has reached the point of satisfaction, their need or longing for another ceases. Unfortunately, many Christians, especially women never reach this place, whether it be inside or outside the institution of marriage.

It has taken my entire life to figure out that complete fulfillment cannot be found in a man. From relationship to relationship, from Marquis to Kenneth, I have realized it is senseless to attempt to find fulfillment in another person. It was not until I came to know Jesus in a personal relationship and discovered He could be whomever I needed that I moved closer to true fulfillment. Now, don't misunderstand me. Just because I have become satisfied in my relationship with the Lord, doesn't mean I have stop desiring male companionship. The devil is a liar! According to Genesis 3:16, God placed the desire within us for a husband. The problem comes when we feel as though we cannot function without the presence of a mate.

In this section, we will look closely at how we can obtain contentment within an intimate relationship with the Lord. We will also look at some great women of the Bible who went through great lengths to obtain the type of pleasure that a relationship with Jesus could only provide. As you begin to read this section, set your mind and spirit to do what is necessary to be used for the purpose God has destined you to fulfill.

God's Orchestra

When I was in 7th grade, I can remember the excitement I had about getting into the band and playing an instrument. I had chosen to play the clarinet in my school's beginning band; and believe me, we sounded like a bunch of beginners. At times, you could hear more air than notes being played. Since we were beginners, when we didn't perfect something as quickly as we thought we should've, we became pretty frustrated. The one thing that kept the band going was the encouraging words from the band director. She knew the potential each one of us had if only we didn't allow the frustrations of learning to discourage us. By the end of the year, our sound was much more polished and refined. We had endured some written and oral test to prove we had learned what was required. Though each band member put in many hours of practice, we could not be any better than the person who was over us, our conductor.

God has called each one of us to be instruments in the orchestra in which He is the conductor. If God is the conductor, it is He who will instruct us when to start and stop "playing". No outside forces should dictate how or when we play our instruments; only the conductor has that power. When the time comes for us to produce sound from our instruments, only the composer is qualified to tell us a particular piece of "sheet music" is to be played in B-flat or C-sharp. This is very important to remember because if we do not listen for the instructions from the Composer, the Holy Ghost, we could be playing the right song in the wrong key. The affects of a song being played in the wrong key can be detrimental to the audience because they will not receive what the conductor intended.

Men and Women of God, we have all been called to a certain ministry in the Body of Christ. However, it is imperative that after we are called we wait on God to choose us, see Matthew 20:16. For example, just because you have recognized the call to evangelize upon your life doesn't mean you immediately begin to run tent revivals. There is a testing, a proving and a pruning you must endure. Also, you must make sure you are playing the right instrument. Why in the world would I attempt to play the soprano saxophone when I was trained to play the clarinet? Likewise, if God has anointed you to be a Sunday school teacher, why would you attempt to be an usher? You are working outside of your calling and you could possibly be playing some wrong notes! Please don't fall into the trap of fulfilling a position in the church because man placed you where God didn't call you. It is better to obey God than man! Once you have come to the conclusion that you are playing the right instrument, wait for the Holy Ghost, the composer, to instruct you on what key you need to play in. In any area of ministry we have the ability to provoke change, so our every move and word needs to be anointed. There is life and death located in that untamable flapping muscle you read about earlier. We truly need the Holy Ghost to help us to control our tongues!

In everything we do we need to make sure our earnest desire is for God to be glorified. Before you sing, usher, preach or teach examine yourself and check your motives. Ask yourself, "Am I doing this to glorify God or to magnify myself?" The main thing I want you to get is this: Our objective should be to save a dying world, heal the broken hearted, set the captive free and to open prison doors. That is it. We don't have time to fight over positions or to be jealous of the pastor's wife. The schisms in the Body need to cease! We are many members of the same body. God doesn't need 200 legs, 55 arms and 150 pairs of eyes. That is an unbalanced body and a jacked up Church! So let's commit ourselves to working in the areas God has called and chosen us for and use that ministry to connect with other believers. Though our strategies may be different, the end result of empowering the Body of Christ to recruit new band members should be the same!

Questions to Ponder

1. Do I know what ministry God has called me to? If yes, what is it?

_____

_____

_____

_____

_____

_____

2. Am I effectively working in this ministry? If no, why not?

_____

_____

_____

_____

_____

_____

3. How can I make sure my motives for being in ministry are pure?

_____

_____

_____

_____

_____

_____

Chapter Fourteen

Finding Comfort in Failure

"Who comforts us in all tribulation, that we may be
able to comfort those who are in trouble, with
the comforts with which we ourselves are
comforted by God," (II Cor. 1:4).

In May of 2000, I was asked to speak at a women's retreat
with the title of this chapter as my topic. I struggled in my natural
mind with this topic because I couldn't fathom how it was possible
to obtain comfort within life's failures. I studied and prayed, prayed
and studied, but it didn't seem like I was receiving any
clarification concerning this topic. Once I stopped trying to
conceive what God wanted me to grasps with my finite mind, I
obtained an understanding of what finding comfort in failure really
means.

To comfort means to gladden or to console. Failure signifies
non-performance, or the inability to produce a desired outcome.
With this in mind, we can conclude that when a person is
experiencing comfort in their failure, it doesn't mean they are
stagnant or complacent in the fact they have failed. What it does
mean is regardless of what a person has experienced, they refuse
to allow an obstacle to determine their fate. No one delights in
being unsuccessful; we all desire to excel in everything we

attempt. Unfortunately, we are prone to make a mistake and/or fail because we dwell in bodies of flesh.

> "For I know that in me (that is, in my flesh) nothing
> good dwells; for to will is present with me, but how
> to perform what is good I do not find." (Rom. 7:18).

However, since we have made a conscious decision to accept the Lord as our personal Savior, our lives should not be governed by the flesh but by the Spirit.

> "Therefore, if any man be in Christ, he is
> a new creation; old things have passed
> away; behold, all things have become new."
> (II Cor. 5:17).

Our old nature, which includes habits, ways of thinking, attitudes, etc., is to be transformed into the very image of God.

The very phrase "Comfort in Failure" seems to be an oxymoron because it does not make any sense! Sometimes we are limited in our understanding of God because we tend to place restrictions on a God who is not bound by time or space. That is why the Bible says, "Let this mind me in you which was also in Christ Jesus," Philippians 2:5. When we realize our condition (a failure) is not our conclusion (final destination), we can use our failures as stepping-stones instead of stumbling blocks!

Being in a State of Fallen

Some years ago, there was a commercial which advertised the Medical Alert Bracelet (MAB). The MAB is a device used by individuals who have a serious illness. In the time of an emergency, the patient could notify 911 by simply pushing a button. In the commercial, an elderly lady had fallen on the floor and exclaimed, "I have fallen and I can't get up!" I can remember the jokes and ridicule this commercial evoked as a result of a person being in distress. Even though the commercial was dramatized, the situation could occur in real life.

Unfortunately, this is how the devil sees the Body of Christ: In a state of fallen with the ability to get up but because the situations surrounding our circumstances seem enormous, we decide it is impossible for us to rise above whatever we face. However, I came to challenge you! Whatever thing the devil has set in your life to destroy you has actually been designed by God to push you into your promised blessing!

Now, before we go any further, I want everyone to close their eyes and think of all the things you know God has promised you which have not come to pass. Now I ask you, "How bad do you want it?" Mark chapter 5 speaks of a woman who had an issue of blood for twelve years. In addition, Luke 13 speaks of a woman who was bent over for eighteen years. These women waited for a length for time for their healing. However, the key to this is that they persevered for what they wanted. How long are you willing to pursue God? The proof of true desire is birthed through an earnest pursuit. Do you have the tenacity it takes to pursue God earnestly to receive what you know is yours?

The Story of Hannah

Scripture Reference: I Samuel 1:1-20

The Scripture text begins listing the ancestry of Elkanah, a Hebrew who had two wives, Peninnah and Hannah. Polygamy, the practice of having more than one wife or husband, was permitted during this time. At any rate, it normally caused problems, as in this story.

A woman during the Old Testament times who could not bear children was viewed as being cursed by God. Because of this label, Hannah felt she was less than a woman and a total failure.

Since Peninnah could have children, Hannah had a constant reminder of her inability to reproduce. Hannah could have allowed her situation to cause her to become bitter towards Elkanah, Peninnah and even God. Hannah realized she was a woman of destiny and even though her inability to conceive produced a feeling of failure, she turned her feelings of failure into a state of desperation which led her right into her miracle. Think of those Peninnah's in your life. Those things which mock the very fact you trust in a God you cannot see with the physical eye. Those things that desire to provoke you to move outside of God's timetable. Will you allow your Peninnah to drive you away from getting closer to God or will you allow your Peninnah to drive you into a hot pursuit for the very face of God with an attitude like Jacob, "I will not let You go unless you bless me," (Gen. 32:26).

Hannah's desire for a child drove her to the tabernacle; the house of God. If we cannot come into contact with God anywhere else, we should be able to commune with Him in a place that has been set-aside for Him to dwell. Nevertheless, we find that there are not enough people of God to evoke the presence of God. If everyone who attended church acted like the Church God has called us to be, then instead of God coming on occasion, His presence would abound continually. If God is in you then you have no need to look for Him.

In this text, Hannah is described as being bitter in soul and as a result, she prayed in anguish. There is something to be said about a woman who prays with bulldog tenacity. No matter how long it takes or what measures she has to go through, this type of woman will not let go of the throne room of God until she receives her answer. If you want some changes to occur in your life and church, gather some women together who will go before God sincerely and boldly! The effectual fervent prayers of the righteous woman do avail much. Because of Hannah's deep desire and pure motive, God granted her request and she conceived a male child.

Dealing With Failures

When we fail, we become exposed. Henceforth, we are naked and ashamed before God. For instance, Adam and Eve. The devil would take delight in our destruction. Nevertheless, we have to make a conscious decision not to be deceived by his well-configured schemes. Regardless of how we mess up, the Bible declares "All things will work together for the good of them who love God and who are the called according to Hs purpose," (Rom. 8:28).

Failures will do one of two things. First, as a result of being naked before God, we realize our humanity and God's divinity. Secondly, failures magnify our human weakness which is where God's strength is to be made perfect. The main thing to remember is to not allow your failures to stunt your growth in God. The best remedy I can give you is to choose to turn your failures into victories is by acquiring these attributes:

1. **Faith** in God and not on what you can see, (Heb. 11:1).
2. **Tenacity** or the ability to stick to a thing and not giving up in the face of adversity, (Gal. 6:9)
3. **Praise** should be a lifestyle not a chore. We should get in a habit of giving God continual thanks, no matter what we face, (Ps. 42:5).
4. **Longing**, a deep yearning for the things of God and an earnest desire to be in His will, (Ps. 42:1).
5. **Focus** on the conclusion and not the condition, (II Cor. 4:17-18).
6. **Recognize** that it is all about God, and not about you, (II Cor. 4:7).
7. **Desperation** is the place you come to when you will go through whatever you must to get what God has for you, (II Cor. 4:8-9).

If you strive to obtain all of these characteristics and possess them, you can walk in the authority given to you through the Holy Ghost and turn all of failures into victories!

Questions to Ponder

1. How have my past or current failures caused me not to walk in victory?

_____

_____

_____

_____

_____

_____

2. What are the "Peninnah's" in my life? What can I do to put them in their place?

_____

_____

_____

_____

_____

_____

3. In Jeremiah 9:17-18, a call is made for the "mourning women and the skillful wailing women" to pray on behalf of a nation. With this in mind, how do I view my own prayer life? How can I attain what is necessary to provoke a change in my life through my prayers?

_____

_____

_____

_____

_____

_____

Chapter Fifteen

Broken at the Feet of Jesus

"And there is no creature hidden from His sight,
but all things are naked and open to the eyes of
Him to whom we must give account," (Heb. 4:13).

The Book of Mark is the shortest of the four Gospels however, it tells more about the actions rather than the teachings of Jesus. It was written by John Mark, who wrote the Gospel while in Rome, to the Roman culture. Mark emphasizes the deity of Jesus and the redemptive nature of His death and resurrection. While all of the events recorded in this book are significant, I believe the story of the woman who anointed Jesus is the most notable.

Scripture Reference: Mark 14:1-9, Matthew 26:6-16
and John 12:1-8

The anointing of Jesus at Bethany by an unnamed woman is an introduction to what is called the Passion Narrative. This event was set in the midst of Passover and the Feast of the Unleavened Bread. The Jewish religious leaders, the Sanhedrin, had decided to capture Jesus and put Him to death. However, due to their fear of an uprising, they did not want to seize Him openly.

While in Bethany, Jesus was being honored with a meal in the home of Simon the leper. While sitting at the table, a woman came having an alabaster flask of very costly oil. Alabaster was considered to be the best material to preserve ointments. Since Mary chose to break this costly flask, the spectators responded in an upheaval. However, they failed to realize, as did Cain, true worship requires a sacrifice from the heart. Men and Women of God, the time has come for us to stop looking at a person's form in worship. Attending church for a long time can teach a person the correct mannerisms. Nevertheless, God's eyes pierces through our flesh and sees the part of us which really matters, the heart! Be careful on who you call spiritual just because of the way they act during praise and worship. In the first division of Samuel, we are reminded not to be so concerned with the outward man that we neglect the inward man. The Body of Christ will miss out on a lot of valuable individuals with priceless gifts and talents who are anointed if we are not led by the Spirit instead of the eyes of the flesh.

When Mary came before Jesus and broke the alabaster box, I believe the box actually represented her. She realized at that point that she, in herself was nothing in the presence of the Messiah. So here she was with all of her insufficiencies, before Jesus who knew no sin. As stated before, when we enter into God's presence, our failures are made evident. This woman was so awesome in that while all eyes were on her, she acted as if she and Jesus were the only two in the room. That is what I call being naked and not ashamed. When you decide it is imperative that you receive something from God, you don't care where you are or who sees you!

The main text in Mark tells us that this woman poured the oil on Jesus' head and has anointed His body for burial. As Mary began to worship the Lord, she came into contact with deity and she realized her humanity. Since worship is man's way of adoring God for who He is, I believe this event reminded Jesus of who He was in relation to God the Father. In lieu of what He was about to face, i.e. dying on the cross, He could not lose sight of His purpose or who He represented. When we worship God, we tell Him how awesome He is. We also show Him our appreciation for His willingness to give Himself in spite of ourselves. God is a God of compassion; He has always looked out for us. The very least we can do is give Him what is due to Him!

As previously stated, Mark records that this woman anointed the head of Jesus; Matthew records the exact same thing. However, John's account of this event states the woman anointed the feet of Jesus. I believe the anointing of Jesus' head first bears much more significance. In Ephesians 5:23, Paul refers to Christ as being the Head of the Church. In comparison, I Corinthians 12 says the Church is like a body with many members. When one takes a visual picture of the human body, one can see that the head is the uppermost part of the body. The head houses the brain which dictates the functions of the rest of the body. When Mary anointed the head of Jesus, His neck, arms, legs, etc. were also being anointed for His burial. In order for the will of God to be carried out, Jesus' will had to be put to death. In order for us as children of God to be equipped to fulfill our divine destiny, our bodies must also be put to death. God will not anoint living flesh because no flesh can glory in His presence, (I Cor. 1:29). So if you want to be anointed, you have to die. It is uncomfortable and it may even hurt, but its effects are eternal!

The Cost of Being Broken

When God breaks up things in our lives, it is very painful. If you really want to be used by God, there is a price you have to pay. There are some things about your past life which will have to be exposed in order for healing to take place in you so you can be an effective minister to others who may be dealing with the same issue(s). God wants to bring forth healing within you so you can be a mouthpiece for Him. We'll deal more with healing our past issues in Chapter 20.

Questions to Ponder

1. Have I allowed myself to become broken at the feet of Jesus? If yes, what was the end result? If no, why not?

_____

_____

_____

_____

_____

_____

2. What things can I give God from my "Alabaster Box"?

_____

_____

_____

_____

_____

_____

3. What lesson can I learn from this woman who anointed Jesus at Bethany?

_____

_____

_____

_____

_____

_____

Chapter Sixteen

"In Order to Get What Ruth Got, You Must Do What Ruth Did!"

"For you, bretheren, have been called to liberty:
only do not use liberty as an opportunity for the
flesh, but through love serve one another," (Gal. 5:13).

Scripture Reference: The Book of Ruth

The story of Ruth takes place in the latter period of Judges, when everyone did what was right in his own eyes, see Judges 21:25. This chaotic atmosphere was present because there was no king in Israel. No matter how much we think we can do things on our own, the covering we receive from leadership is necessary. Eve had Adam, Israel had Moses and others and the disciples had Jesus. Leadership is fundamental!

This story of Ruth and Naomi is one of the most romantic accounts in the Bible. You may have even said to yourself, "I desire a Boaz or Ruth." However, before you read the meat of this chapter, I really want you to consider whether or not you are ready to do what it takes to not only obtain a Ruth or Boaz, but also what it takes to keep one. Marriage is much more than looks, an image and flesh. Marriage is a ministry and ministry is a sacrifice. If you are not ready and willing to minister to your perspective husband or wife spiritually (first and foremost), mentally, physically, socially and financially then you are not really ready to be married.

The first thing I would like to focus on is the death of Naomi's husband and sons. In the previous chapter, we learned it is critical that something in our lives die in order for us to be anointed. The Scripture text says the death of Naomi's loved ones caused her to be bitter. In essence, she thought her current condition was to be her conclusion. She did not realize she was being molded to receive something great. When God causes certain people to be taken away from us for a season or indefinitely, it is hurtful. Nevertheless, when we realize God has desired for us to come up to another level in Him, we should be encouraged and trust in Him enough to know He knows what He is doing. If you are pressing toward level ten, your level three friends will not be able to flow with where God is trying to take you. For every level there is there are more devils to fight. Don't you want people in your life who will be able to stand with you and not run from you in the face of adversity?

After the death of her husband and sons, Naomi returned to her homeland of Judah, along with her daughters-in-law Ruth and Orpah. At the point of their arrival, she tells the young maidens to return to their mother's house to find husbands because there was probably no hope for them to find spouses in Judah. Every time I hear this story taught, I notice that people love to look down on Orpah for leaving and returning home. I only wish the things in my life which were obstacles to me receiving those things God has promised me would move that easily. There was only one Boaz and one inheritance to be redeemed. It was evident whom God had chosen to fulfill what He had purposed.

> "Entreat me not to leave you. Or to turn back
> from following after you; for wherever you go,
> I will go; and wherever you lodge, I will lodge;
> your people shall be my people, and your God,
> my God." (1:16).

Ruth saw something in Naomi she herself desired. In addition, she realized there was nothing for her in her mother's house. Sometimes God will require us to move from our areas of comfort in order for us to receive what He has. You can choose to return to what is familiar like Orpah did; however, your choices will be limited and absent of the true and living God. One other interesting fact I'd like to shed light on. Naomi refers to herself as being full when she left Moab, but returning empty (verse 21). My, my, my! What Naomi failed to realize, as we do, is the first step to being filled is becoming empty. How can God fill a vessel that already contains substance? For example, the widow who only had a jar of oil in II Kings 4. The prophet Elisha told her to gather empty vessels and pour what she had into them. Once she moved in obedience from the word spoken by the prophet, God took what she had and multiplied it. All God is looking for is an empty vessel!

A Meeting With Destiny

At this point, we find Naomi and Ruth settling in Judah. Since Naomi's husband and son's had died, their source of income had also died. Naomi had legal rights to the land her husband owned but because of customs, she needed a man to redeem the land for her. Her plight was to find the next of kin to marry Ruth, since she was beyond the age of childbearing. Ruth felt inclined to take care of Naomi so she was willing to place the needs of her mother-in-law before her own. Ruth was a self-less individual.

By the instructions of Naomi, Ruth began to glean after the reapers in the field of Boaz, and HE noticed HER; she was not trying to make herself known. She knew her position as a woman of God. She was noticed while serving; need I say anymore? Once Boaz discovered who she was, he gave her instructions to only glean in his field and she followed what she was told. This shows that Ruth was humble and not domineering. She appreciated Boaz's willingness to look after her for she had found favor in his sight. Ruth was also unique. Out of all the maidservants that were gleaning in Boaz's field that day, he noticed her. There is something to be said about living a lifestyle of holiness. I don't want to get ahead of myself, but the flesh dictates the lives of too many people in the Church body as it is. Some of us have already specified to God the physical attributes we would like our mates to have. What happens when his six-pack becomes a ten? Is the love lost because the outer shell has changed? We must change our perspective. I believe God knows what is attractive to you, so it is safe for me to say He will not give you someone you cannot stand to look at. Nevertheless, the flesh must not lead us when choosing a mate. In other words, we must go "spiritual" when it comes to choosing someone who we will share the rest of our lives with.

When Ruth returned to Naomi and filled her in on the events of the day, Naomi knew this was not a meeting of chance but of destiny. In chapter one of our text, we read how Naomi became bitter because she felt the lord had afflicted her. Now she realized it was not a permanent situation but a spiritual set up! Hallelujah! Just think, if God were to bless us with the things He has promised us on our terms, we would not appreciate anything. God's power would be reduced to that of a Jeannie; we need to loose this rub the bottle and get what I want mentality. We must learn to seek God's face and learn who He is. The treasures of God are found in His face, not in His hand.

After Ruth told Naomi about her day, Naomi gave Ruth some additional instructions to prepare herself for meeting Boaz. This included washing and anointing herself and putting on her best garment. She could not go before the man of God any kind of way and expect him to desire her. There is nothing wrong with a little makeup, perfume and nice clothes. Women as well as men should represent God first and ourselves second. Ruth knew by following Naomi, a woman of wisdom, she would be led in the right direction. I think it is critical for every young woman to have an older woman as a mentor. Regardless of our past, we do not know everything. Who better to teach us than a woman who has been where we are and is currently where we would like to be. For a Scripture reference, see Titus 2:3-5.

Ruth's instructions were to go to the threshing floor where Boaz would be watching over his grain. Once Boaz lied down, she was to uncover his feet and lie down beside him; and this is exactly what she did. When Boaz realized who was at his feet and Ruth explained what she wanted from him, he was inclined to respond. When you move within God's timing with God's man or woman, you won't have to question whether or not it is God. When we allow our steps to be ordered by God and not the desires of our flesh, we'll be able to recognize God more efficiently.

Boaz explained to Ruth that he would be happy to marry her, however, there was a relative closer than him and he should have the opportunity to redeem the land if he chose to. When Boaz told the close relative about the land, he was eager to redeem it. Yet, when he was informed of having to marry Ruth to perpetuate the name of Elimelech, he declined. Boaz was then free to marry Ruth. Because God had sanctified and divinely orchestrated this union, Boaz and Ruth's offspring Obed produced Jesse who produced David. This makes them a part of the royal lineage of Jesus Christ.

What Did Ruth Have?

One of the first things recognizable about Ruth is she was not afraid to make a covenant or commitment. She made a solemn agreement with Naomi to not leave her side until death separated them. She was a woman of her word and integrity. People in general value someone they can trust and depend on. No one likes a flaky, unstable individual who changes with the wind. Amen, somebody! Next, Ruth wasn't afraid to work! Is that a foreign word? I have never seen a more lazy generation than my own; everyone wants a hand out. I apologize if you take offense to that, but it is so true. It seems that my generation wants to be catered to and taken care of. We must be a little more responsible and take care of ourselves. If I am not mistaken, the Bible still declares that if a person doesn't work, they don't eat (II Thess. 3:10). God will not bless the lazy! Discontentedly, many of us take a "savior" mentality in regards to the ideas we have about marriage. A man is not sent from God to take care of a woman's financial dilemmas and repair her scarred emotions. If you don't have anything to offer to a man of God, why should he want to be with you? After the flesh is satisfied, what is next? Come on girlie-girls, we won't spend the bulk of our marriage lives in the sheets! If you are relying solely on your looks to attract someone, you will be sadly disappointed. Your hips may draw him, but it will be your spirit that keeps him! The true men of God should be shouting "Glory" right about now!

Another characteristic of Ruth is she was willing to take correction from others. Oh, oh, here is another hot topic! I am about to tell you something you may not be aware of. You don't know everything! I know you are in ultra shock, but listen a moment. We need not get offended when someone comes to us, in love, to correct us or teach us something. We could gain so much insight from those older and more seasoned than ourselves if our heads were not so big. Trust me, Boaz wants a teachable woman. If you possess all of these characteristics together, they would make you a Proverbs 31 woman.

If you obtain all the characteristics of a Ruth, you will attract the likes of a Boaz who will be a man of God, protector, provider, a watchman for your soul, a man of honor and integrity. He will also be respected by those in his community, which includes his family, church and place of employment. Boaz is also a giver, lover and most importantly a kinsmen redeemer!

Food for Thought

It is not easy to acquire the attributes of a Ruth. To some degree, it may seem impossible. However, if your focus is on the fact that your life is not your own, but God's, you will place yourself in a position to where He is able to mold you into the woman He has destined you to become. It may be a long process, so I encourage you not to get frustrated. Whenever God does bless you with a mate, you want to be ready for his/her arrival; let God do the patchwork in the meantime!

Questions to Ponder

1. How do I feel about commitment? Has my past experiences clouded my view of it?

_____

_____

_____

_____

_____

_____

2. Do I have a "Naomi" in my life? If yes, what have I learned from her?

_____

_____

_____

_____

_____

_____

3. What are the (5) most important qualities I desire in a mate? Why are these the most important aspects of a mate for me?

_____

_____

_____

_____

_____

_____

Chapter Seventeen

The Woman With the 'Issue'

"Not that I have already attained or am already
perfected; but I press on, that I may lay hold of
that for which Christ Jesus has also laid hold of
me," (Phil. 3:12).

Scripture Reference: Luke 8:40-48

At this point in Scripture, we find Jesus at the peak of his
ministry. Earlier in this chapter of Luke, we find Jesus bringing
deliverance to a man filled with thousands of demons. As a
result, the word was out about the power He possessed which
explains the multitude that welcomed Him in verse 40. The
anxious crowd wanted to see what Jesus would do next. Enter
Jairus.

A ruler of the synagogue named Jairus, fell on his face and
petitioned Jesus to come to his house to heal his dying daughter.
In response, Jesus went into the direction of this man's house. In
all the upheaval, a woman having an issue of blood for twelve
years was in the crowd. She evidently heard about this Man who
could heal the sick, raise the dead and feed 5,000. Surely, He
could do something for her! For her, it was worth a try, seeing she
had spent her life savings on doctor after doctor, only to leave

her in a worse condition. Because of her condition, she was probably physically weak and despondent. I could only imagine how she felt. Just think, PMS everyday for twelve long, exhausting years. My God!

As if this wasn't bad enough, according to the law she was to be regarded as unclean, see Leviticus 15:25-27. Also, anyone or anything she came into contact with was to be regarded as unclean. This woman took an enormous risk, because I am sure everyone in the city knew who she was. But isn't it funny that no one pointed her out in the crowd? No, it was not fate; it was a date with destiny!

Getting In a Press

The Scripture says that as Jairus led Jesus to his house, the multitude thronged him, verse 42. This simply means the crowd was so great until the people were pressed together. Jairus probably had to use great force to get through the people; with this in mind, think about this woman. Luke records that she came from behind Jesus and touched the border of His garment. Now, realize the border is not located around the collar or sleeve, but the hem. That means she was on her hands and knees, trying to get to Jesus. What drove her to this state, you ask? I'd call it sheer desperation! She more than likely began to think about all the money she had spent to no avail. Then she started to reminisce about how much she has had to suffer with this issue of blood. Lastly, she recalled episodes which occurred in town where she was humiliated by being called "unclean". The crowd didn't matter to her; what people thought about her had no relevance. Though she may have been physically weak, the adrenaline rush her thoughts produced caused her to gain the strength she needed to get through the crowd. So, she commenced to press through the masses and with every move, her faith was increased.

The Power of the Touch

> "(the woman) came from behind and touched
> the border of His garment. And immediately
> her flow of blood stopped," (verse 44).

Can you say "immediately"? As soon as the faith of this woman touched Jesus, her 'issue' was over! No, it didn't decrease over a period of time; it just stopped! Glory to God! But wait, that wasn't all that took place. She touched Jesus with such desperation and faith until His undivided attention was hers. The reason she had His attention was because power went from Him into her. And you know once you come into contact with the Lord, nothing in your life will ever be the same. When the woman saw that Jesus knew what had taken place, she came before Him trembling. This demonstrates she reverenced Jesus for who He was. As a result, He told her "your faith has made you well. Go in peace," (verse 48).

"The Issue"

For this woman, the issue was blood; so I ask you, What is your issue? What thing have you been dealing with year after year without resolution? What condition has had you up crying many tears in the midnight hour and left you pacing the floor during the day? You have talked to your family, friends and pastor and still you have come up empty. You've exhausted all of your natural resources, but have you touched God with what concerns you? If you really want to stop the flow of your issue, take the following cues from this woman.

A. She persevered for her healing.

    1. Hundreds were pushing in the crowd, but only she pressed through.

2. Many were pushing Him, but only she touched Him. There is a difference between a push and a touch.

B. She had faith.

1. Though weak, weary and dishearten, she knew Jesus could heal her.
2. She did not wait for Jesus to lay hands on her; she went after what she wanted.

C. She didn't allow her past disappointments to dictate her future healing.

1. She spent all she had.
2. She went to many physicians and none could cure her condition.

In essence, the conclusion here is that this woman had perseverance, faith, desire and tenacity. If you possess all of these elements, you have the ability to touch Jesus. Hebrews 4:15 informs us, "For we do not have a High Priest who cannot sympathize with our weaknesses, but was in all points tempted as we are, yet without sin." Jesus knows what it is to experience pain and hurt; He has already been where we are. He is waiting on you to touch Him with whatever concerns you.

Questions to Ponder

1. What is my 'issue'?

_____

_____

_____

_____

_____

_____

2. What sources have I exhausted in trying to stop the flow of my 'issue'?

    _____

    _____

    _____

    _____

    _____

    _____

3. Have I ever touched Jesus with the feeling of my infirmities? How or why not?

    _____

    _____

    _____

    _____

    _____

    _____

Chapter Eighteen

Go, and Get a Drink!

"Blessed are those who hunger and thirst for
righteousness, for they shall be filled," (Matt. 5:6)

Scripture Reference: John 4:1-30

I must admit, of all the women I have discussed, the Samaritan woman is my favorite. Maybe it's because she was the topic of my first sermon; or could it be that I identify with her search for fulfillment so much until I see a reflection of myself in her? I think the second question is my answer!

At the beginning of this chapter, we find Jesus having an altercation with the religious Pharisees. Somehow, they had heard Jesus was baptizing more people than John. To keep down confusion, He left Judea in route to Galilee. Nevertheless, because of the ancient feud between the Jews and the Samaritans, no orthodox Jew would pass through Samaria (Macartney 112). This meant that a Jew would have to take a round about journey to reach Galilee. In verse 4, John says, "But He needed to go through Samaria." This lets me know that regardless of the danger or turmoil which may surround your situation, Jesus is willing to come directly to our wells to quench our thirst. What an awesome God we serve!

The Scripture records that when the woman came to draw water, Jesus said to her "Give me a drink," (verse 7). He already knew this woman would be there, that day and at the sixth hour. Being who she was, she was puzzled by His request. In response, He said these words:

> "If you only knew the gift of God and who it is
> who says to you, 'Give me a drink,' you would
> have asked Him, and He would have given you
> living water," (verse 10).

That statement went right over her head. Since she was not born again and lacked spiritual discernment, she had no idea what Jesus was offering her. She proceeded by looking for a natural device, something to draw with, to address her spiritual need for living water. Jesus responds.

> "Whoever drinks of this water will thirst again, but
> whoever drinks of the water that I shall give him
> will never thirst. But the water that I shall give him
> will become in him a fountain of living water springing
> up into everlasting life," (verses 13-14).

And again, she missed it! And guess what? We would've missed it too! The reason I know this is because she's thinking, "Man, if He could give me some water that would cause me not to thirst again, I want it!" We should realize that our attempt to handle a spiritual situation by natural means does not work!

Before she could have this water of eternal life, she had to confront the presence of sin in her life. When Jesus asked her where her husband was, she said she didn't have one. I can imagine she became a little hesitant about this stranger inquiring about her personal life. When Jesus exposed the fact that He knew she had been married five times and was currently shacking, she made a conversation change. Isn't that just like us? When we get uncomfortable about discussing certain things, we'll change the subject in a heartbeat! Jesus wasn't ignorant to her methods; however, He desired to show her His divine motive. The next conversational piece was in reference to worship.

> "Our fathers worshipped on this mountain, and you Jews say that in Jerusalem is the place where one ought to worship. Woman, believe me, the hour is coming when you will neither on this mountain nor in Jerusalem, worship the Father. You worship what you do not know; we know what we worship, for salvation is of the Jews. But the hour is coming, and now is, when the true worshippers will worship the Father in spirit and in truth; for the Father is seeking such to worship Him. God is a spirit, and those who worship Him must worship in spirit and in truth," (verses 20-24).

The Samaritan woman then inquires about the formality of worship. In response, Jesus informed her that she was worried about the wrong thing. It is not where you worship, but Who you worship. At this point, Jesus was able to offer salvation and forgiveness for her sins.

Why Are You Still Thirsty?

It is amazing to me as to why a person who comes to God and sees what He can do, would make the decision to allow the things of the world to intrigue them. I mean we have tried men/women and sex and it has left us feeling guilty and worthless. Drugs and alcohol leave you antsy, frigidity and paranoid. Successful jobs, elaborate houses and fine cars do nothing for your self-esteem. What Jesus has is first of all free. Can you say free? Then, after you give Him you, there is nothing to feel guilty about. Jesus did not give this woman a list of do's and don'ts; He just required her to confront her present and make it her past and seek Him for herself to obtain the intimate fellowship found in worship.

Initially, this woman did not understand that before she could get her thirst quenched, she had to confess the presence of sin in her life. The mere fact that she asked Jesus for a drink before she did this shows she attempted to receive the benefits of a joint heir without being adopted into the royal family. Having an intimate relationship with God is contingent upon us dismissing sin from our lives. Sin places enmity between us and God, so there is no way He will dwell where sin is.

Once sin has been confronted, we must move to seek a personal relationship with the Lord. The main idea to see here is the physical place of worship is not important. The critical aspect to remember is the position of your heart. In order to worship God in spirit, we must possess His Spirit. There is nothing to praising God; the animals can do that. However, when we move into worship, we move out of self and allow the spirit of God in you to take control. Think of it this way. The Book of Psalm records that God inhabits the praises of His people. In order for God to live in our praise He comes to where we are. But, when we worship God in the spirit of God, He takes us to where He lives. That is why no flesh can glory in His sight; we must have His spirit!

Food for Thought

Like many of us, this woman had a thirst that six men could not quench. It seems elementary to say this, but sometimes I think we fail to remember that all we need is found in a relationship with God. We should stop looking for the wells when what we really desire are the fountains of living water which lead us to eternal life.

Questions to Ponder

1. What has my inner desire led me to thirst after in the past?

    _____

    _____

    _____

    _____

    _____

    _____

2. Do I sometimes attempt to divert the attention from myself to avoid self-confrontation?

    _____

    _____

    _____

    _____

    _____

    _____

3. Am I eligible to worship God in spirit and in truth? Why or why not?

    _____

    _____

    _____

    _____

    _____

    _____

PART IV

Single

"For My Priest"

Oh man of purpose and Godly insight,
Oh man of the highest esteem, will you enter into my
life?
I am captivated by your words,
Your ability to yield uncompromising advice,
These attributes only confirm that you are a true example
of Christ.
When analyzing this thing called love, I became
extremely weary,
My past relationships caused me to be a quite leery.
The thought of coming into contact with my Boaz never
seemed to me a reality,
Until you came into my life and caused me to inhabit a
real-life fantasy.
Oh man of valor, it is you God has ordained for my life,
And soon it will be revealed that I am Ruth, your virtuous
wife.

Chapter Nineteen

Living Single

"and you are complete in Him, who is the
head of all principality and power," (Col. 2:10).

Up to this point, you have read about subjects dealing with
being saved, sanctified and satisfied. The point I want to stress in
this book is that we should yearn to be saved, sanctified and satisfied
men and women who just happen to be single. Our salvation,
sanctification and satisfaction should not be based on us being single
or married. It however, should be based upon the fact that we are
men and women who are willing to pursue God at any cost and by
any means, no matter whom we are dating, engaged or married to. A
man or woman should not define how we feel about ourselves. We
must stop allowing others to determine our self-esteem.

Me, Myself and I

For the past twenty-nine years of my life, I have been actively
living without a significant other. If I were of the world, I'd probably
sing this golden oldie by the old school R & B group, Cameo:

"I'm living the single, single, single, . . . life!"

To me, being single means not married! When you fill out an

application for employment, there is no space to check for dating or engaged. Being single can be quite a tedious lifestyle, especially if you are not content in being single. To increase the intensity of my state, I've seen my brother, sister and friends get married and have children before me. Oh, joy! When this started happening, I wondered, "God, what is wrong with me? Am I not desirable? What is the deal?" Now, you know when you ask God sincere questions, no matter how trivial they may seem He will give you an answer. Whether you like what He has to say is a different story. With God's help, I realized that Ivy was not ready to be any man's wife. In addition, I came to the conclusion that since I was not going to be married for a while, I was single for some reason. And for this cause, I needed to figure out what the purpose was.

Defining Singlehood

Before we can attempt to proceed any further, we must define what it means to be in a state of singleness. Being single means to be able to stand-alone; to be complete with God. It is the act of being set apart to be transformed into a unit with Christ. In I Corinthians 7:25-40, the Apostle Paul addresses the married and unmarried Christian. The first thing Paul makes clear is that God has not given him any specific instructions concerning this issue. However, he believes his responses are inspired by the Holy Spirit. In verses 34-35, Paul states that the unmarried woman is able to focus on the things of God because she is without the care of a family and a household. In turn, she is able to serve the Lord without distraction.

In short, the state of being single is not to be used to think about getting married; nor is it the time to date the nation to narrow down your choices. The most unattractive person to me is the one who acts as if he/she cannot function without the presence of a man or woman in their life. Yes, God did build us to have the desire for one of the opposite sex. However, He did not form us to have this desire control our lives. The most important focus for us as singles is to know the Lord. God desires to have an intimate relationship with us, but since He is a gentleman, He will not force Himself into a position where He is not wanted.

Off Limits!

I've had about four relationships in my life. While none of these young men looked or acted alike, all four relationships followed the same pattern.

1) Boy meets girl
2) Boy begins to date girl
3) Boy says he loves girl
4) Girl falls in love with boy
5) Boy dodges the idea of commitment
6) Relationship comes to screeching halt

For a long time, I thought something was wrong with me. I mean, what was I doing to make the men in my life run from the idea of committing to me. Well, one day while talking to a male acquaintance, the answer to my dilemma hit me like a ton of bricks.

This guy, we'll call Lawrence, told me how at a certain point in his relationship with God, he was attracting the wrong type of women. Everyone he desired to talk to had no interest in him; and the ones who wanted to talk to him, he had no interest in. Later on, a friend of his told him that God had placed an "Off Limits" sign on him and only those who were spiritual could see it. What a revelation to me! After wondering for years why all of my relationships turned sour, I finally realized that God had placed a sign on me which read:

God's Property!
While Being Prepared For
Her Destiny and Purpose
She is
Off Limits!!!

I guess if I were a man I would run with the quickness if I laid eyes on a sign like this. Like Jeremiah, from the time I was born God had plans for me; and He did not need me marrying the wrong man to throw His plans for me off schedule. Stop thinking something is wrong with you; in God's eyes everything maybe right. If we only allow our eyes to focus on what we see in the natural, we'll never gain insight on what God is doing in the spiritual.

> "While we do not look at the things which are
> seen, but at the things which are not seen. For
> the things which are not seen are eternal."
> (II Cor. 4:18).

The Fear of Loneliness

> "Again, if two lie down together, they will keep
> warm; But how can one be warm alone." (Eccl 4:11).

No one likes the thought of being alone, especially if you have grown accustomed to having company all the time. I know this may sound strange, but there is actually fulfillment in being alone. The problem comes when you are in a state of loneliness. Look at the following definitions, according to Webster.

> Alone: solitary; separately.
> Lonely: unfrequented by men; retired; secluded
> from society.

As you can see, being alone is a spiritual position, while being lonely is more of a physical position. Being alone can lead to being lonely; however, being lonely cannot lead to being alone. Let me explain.

When you are alone in a spiritual sense, you make the decision to allow God to separate you from the busyness of your daily activities so that you can consecrate yourself before Him. During this time of separation I am experiencing currently, I am only allowed to go to work and church. That is it! I am allowing God and His will for my life to take precedence over everything and everyone else. This is where God has me right now. I am persuaded to follow His direction because I don't want to suffer for being a child of disobedience. Being alone is not based on who you are or are not with. You can be set alone while being married. All right, I feel compelled to make this clear. If God does place you alone when you are married, that does not mean you have permission to leave your spouse. I just had to make sure we are clear on that; I don't want anyone taking anything I have said out of context. At any rate, being separated has everything to do with where you are in your relationship with the Lord. When you have been placed alone, you do not have time to focus on the fact that you are by yourself. The reason for this is your focus is so wrapped in the things of God until you do not have the time or energy to give thought to anything else.

On the flip side, when you are lonely, you allow the fact that you are not physically with someone to effect your lifestyle. You either decide not to eat or you eat everything that is not tied down. You seclude yourself from family and friends, become depressed and your self-image becomes extremely low. This is nothing but a trick of the enemy and you must not allow him to fool you. The reason I said being alone can lead to being lonely is because the thought of being separated for the purpose of God may initially be a person's primary focus. Then, as time passes on and the state of separation continues, the focus may be taken off of the spiritual aspect and onto the physical position.

In this final section of this book I want you to scrutinize your life as a single Christian. Do you find yourself seeking a mate more than you seek God? Are you consumed with dating and relationships? Are you jealous when your friends flaunt their engagement rings and/or fiancés in front of your face? Be honest with yourself. The only way to place God in the proper perspective is to first deal with where you are now. Let me warn you, we are about to embrace some very heavy situations. I am sure you will find yourself somewhere in the next five chapters. You may be forced to confront old skeletons that you have only hidden and not buried. Allow me to pray for you, before you read any further.

Lord, I intercede for the man or woman who is about to read the next five chapters. God, I thank you for where you have brought him/her from, where you have him/her now, and where you are about to take him/her in the future. God, I pray that he/she will be loosed from every past situation that has attempted to destroy him/her life and dictate him/her destiny. I pray that every stronghold will be pulled down in Jesus' name. Satan, you are a liar and you will not use his/her past to dictate his/her future. I declare that you are, right now, a man or woman of purpose and destiny who will fulfill the call of God on their life. In Jesus name I do pray, Amen.

Chapter Twenty

Healing Past Wounds

"He heals the brokenhearted and binds up
their wounds," (Ps. 147:3).

When I was about six years old, I remember having a big
wheel. One day while riding it, an older girl decided she wanted
to give me some unwanted assistance. She began to pull my big
wheel to make me go faster. Somehow, my feet fell off of the pedals
and hit the concrete faced down. I screamed in anguish for her
to stop because my feet were sweeping the concrete. When my
ride of horror came to an abrupt end, the top of my feet contained
broken skin, bruises and much blood. I cried myself into my
mother's arms but I calmed down once hydro-peroxide and
medicated ointment was applied to my wounds. Once my wounds
were healed, I did ride my big wheel again but I never allowed
myself to be aided because I was afraid of being hurt. Every time
I looked at the top my feet, the scars were my evidence of the
incident however, the pain and anguish was no longer present.
To this day, I still have those scars on my feet.

At one time or another, we have all experienced being hurt;
some more severe than others. Unfortunately, the devil knows we
have been hurt and will use our past painful situations to make
us doubt God's ability to heal us. He will constantly remind us of
being molested at age nine. He will slap you in the face with the

fact that we may have been raped during our teenage years. He will constantly remind you of that homosexual experience you had in college because he knows deep down inside you still struggle with your sexuality. He will also trip you up with incidents of physical and verbal abuse because he knows you are still quite vulnerable in those areas. Why do you think so many men and women fall into the vicious cycles of unhealthy relationships? Generally, it is because past hurts and issues are not completely healed and dealt with before the search for a new man/woman is underway. If we do not allow God to completely heal us before we enter into new relationships, we will attract the same type of companions every time: Those who abuse us and take advantage of our vulnerability.

Have you ever seen a cut or scrape that has not been cleaned properly? As a result, infection sets in and it looks worse than the initial wound. In addition, it takes longer for the wound to heal. Unfortunately, this is how a lot of us look in the spirit. Instead of allowing God to come in and heal our soulish realm, we do patchwork on our wounds by putting an emotional band-aid on it. We figure if it is covered, we don't have to see or deal with it. However, what we don't see is the infection we allow to set in. This is what makes it difficult for us to enter into new relationships; we still have open cuts and bruises and abrasions from the last relationship. So, if you have ever found yourself comparing David to Willie, this is why!

A Father's Love

For the first eight years of my life, I had an active, loving relationship with my father. I can remember him taking me on trips to visit his family in Sanford, Florida. I can also recall him placing me on his lap and calling me his baby girl. I loved my "dada" so much; he could do no wrong in my eyes. Then, without notice, he stopped coming around everyday. Visiting everyday turned into three times a week. Then, three times a month. Next, three times a year and finally it was next to never. I was so distraught over this because I missed my daddy. For the next sixteen years of my life, I found myself looking to relationships with men to gather what I had missed from not having my father in my life. During all this time, I blamed myself for doing something to make my daddy not want to be involved in my life. Then, one-day revelation came from an unlikely source.

Since my dad and I had stopped communicating on a regular basis during my childhood, I didn't have an opportunity to meet all of his siblings. When I transferred from community college to a four-year university, my dad told me one of his brothers was a professor there. I had the chance to speak with him a few times before I left for school and he expressed that he couldn't wait to meet me. Four weeks after I arrived at FAMU, I met my uncle for the first time at age twenty. It was such an exciting and joyous occasion until . . .

As we were talking, my uncle began to tell me about how my dad and his wife came to his college graduation in 1974. I said no, my dad and mom were together then because that's when I was born. See, to my knowledge, my dad had gotten married sometime after he was with my mom. After much debate, I called to ask my mom about this, but she wasn't available at the time. I then called and asked my sister and she told me that my dad was married to his current wife at the time of my birth. I was utterly shaken! All the times I had blamed myself for not being good enough for my dad to love, began to play back in my mind. I was more hurt than angry and I started to cry tears of excruciating anguish and heartfelt pain. My sister could not understand why I was so broken up over this situation. When someone has not walked in your shoes and felt what you have, it is hard for them to relate to certain issues that may devastate you. That is why we should never down play any obstacle a person has to overcome. Since you may have never experienced my test, you have no reason to disregard my testimony. Well, when my mom found out I knew, she called me at school and told me she would be there the next day. I told her it was O.K. and that I wasn't mad at her. She said she was coming anyway. Now that is a mother!

When my mom came, she checked into a hotel and we went to dinner. She initiated the conversation by apologizing to me for having to find out the way that I did. She then proceeded to tell me she didn't find out my dad was married until after I was born. In spite of her knowledge of my dad's marital state, she decided to stay with him because he continued to promise her he would leave his wife and marry her. Unfortunately, weeks turned into months and months turned into years. O.K., let's be real! If a married man says he is going to leave his wife for you, he is lying! Even if he does leave, you will always have to deal with the probability that he will leave you for another woman. Take a stand and do what you know is right. Our God is too good to make us settle for another woman's leftovers. God has some prime rib for you! At this point, my mom decided to severe the relationship because she wanted to live for the Lord. In retaliation, my dad cut me off to get back at my mom for leaving him. What he didn't consider was the effect his actions would have on me. This is why when children are born outside of a marriage, it is important to consider how things will affect the children involved. Stop being so selfish! Stop trying to inflict pain upon your baby's daddy at the expense of your baby! If the relationship is over, God will help you deal with that. That is the easy part. What you don't want is a child who spends the rest of his or her life searching for a father's love in the carnal realm. Please don't allow your emotions to dictate your actions.

Sometimes you hear people say it was difficult for them to receive the love of God when they did not have a father in their life. Well, that is not my testimony! When I realized that God was willing to give me unconditional love with no strings attached, I was overjoyed. Finally, a man who was willing to give me the love I wanted without me having to give something up! However, I still find it difficult to receive love from a man because I don't feel like I deserve it. I have been abused both emotionally and mentally until I still bare wounds from the battle. Unlike natural wounds which heal in days, emotional scars can bleed for a lifetime.

In Need of a Physician

"Those who are well have no need of a
physician, but those who are sick,"
(Matt. 9:12).

After this experience in my life, I was in need of a physician. In addition, it wasn't until a few years ago I realized that me not having my father in my life at those critical times of my development directly affected my dating relationships. I knew God had a lot of operating to do. If I was willing to go under the spiritual scalpel and endure the pain associated with healing, God's work was insurable. Remember, He has never lost a case or misdiagnosed a condition. His accuracy is impeccable.

I really didn't realize how deep my hurt was concerning this issue until I heard Bishop Jakes one Sunday morning. During this sermon, I discovered how my father's inconsistencies and the words he spoke to me turned internal. In addition, the men in my past have exclaimed: "You are too fat for me", "I never loved you", "You are not the type of woman I prayed for", or "You do not fit the image of who I want my wife to be" and the list goes on. I have replayed these words in my mind over and over again until I began to believe them myself. I realize now that this is why I became a performance—oriented woman in my relationships. I thought doing things for the men in my life would be personal insurance and assurance for commitment. Little did I know that I would end up in a deficit. I would buy cologne, write poetry, and cook dinner, among other things, all for the sake of love. At any rate, time after time, equal action was not returned by the men who claimed they were in love with me.

"For the hurt of the daughter of my people I
am hurt. I am mourning; astonishment has
taken hold of me. Is there no balm in Gilead,
Is there no physician there? Why then is there
no recovery for the health of the daughter of
my people?" (Jer. 8:21-22)

Mount Gilead is a mountain located near the Jordan River. Gilead is translated to mean "rocky region". Located in the Mountains of Gilead was a balm or healing agent. So in essence the question Jeremiah asked God was "Is there no healing in those rocky places in our lives? Are you not Jehovah Rapha, the God who heals us?" Healing is available to us and God is our physician. We should make a move to be recovered and restored for He is concerned with our total well being. God is willing to make house calls if you are willing to let Him be your personal physician.

How Do I Heal My Past?

If we have made a conscious decision to be healed of our past hurts, then action must be added to our faith in God's ability to heal us. Faith without works is truly dead. We must cast our cares on Jesus because He cares for us. A song I heard a few years ago gave the perfect remedy in beginning the healing the process: Forget about the past, don't worry about the present and look forward to the future. As I have said before, I don't believe in giving a five-step program. I'm just sharing with you what has worked and is still working for me.

The first thing I had to do was forgive my past. No one ever forgets their painful situations. But, if we allow our Balm in Gilead to heal us, we can effectively forgive our past. In forgiving the past, we will not forget our situations. However, when we think about them, it will not hurt us anymore. Sleepless nights will disappear and tear ducts will dry up. At this point, we become prized trophies displaying the miraculous and rewarding expressions of God's healing power.

The next thing I had to do was forgive those who had hurt me in my past. This is a vital but difficult step, especially when it came to forgiving my dad. I would always throw past issues in his face, which only prolonged my healing process. Until this day, my father and I have not discussed what took place when I was a child. I found myself trying to make him be the father I always wanted, when those years were gone for us. I realized I could not make him fill a position he was not willing to accept. I could no longer base my ability to be healed on whether he would accept his responsibility in hurting me. Regardless of what he did, I wanted to be healed. Lastly, I had to forgive myself. I had to realize that there was nothing that I did or didn't do to make things turn out the way they did. Until I was able to forgive myself, I couldn't effectively forgive others or my experiences. I would always say, "If I would have" or "I should not have"; this only made things more difficult for me.

As a woman, I know we spend a large portion of our lives learning how to be loving, sensitive and altruistic. We generally have a genuine concern about the welfare of others; even those of us who try to act non-chalont. We have these traits instilled into us at an early age. That is why it is nothing for us to go without a new dress so we can provide for our families and households. However, we can still possess these characteristics and be the strong women of God we are called to become. Ask God to heal all of your past wounds. Some of your 'broken skin' and 'bruises' may be severe and they may even contain much 'blood'. Jehovah Rapha will apply His own special hydro-peroxide and medicated ointment. After a while, the pain will disappear and your scars will become your evidence of what you experience, but they won't define who you are!

Questions to Ponder

1. What past issues in my life do I need to experience healing in?

   _____

   _____

   _____

   _____

   _____

   _____

2. How have these open wounds prohibited me from walking in my destiny?

   _____

   _____

   _____

   _____

   _____

   _____

3. Has my relationship with my natural father had a positive or negative influence on my relationship with God? Explain.

   _____

   _____

   _____

   _____

   _____

   _____

Chapter Twenty-One

Relationship Check: Discovering What Love is

"And now abide faith, hope, love, these three
but the greatest of these is love," (I Cor. 13:13).

According to Webster, love is to regard with affection, to like, to delight in, warm affection or fond attachment. If we live our lives with this definition of love as our foundation, we will have a misguided view of what love really is. When we allow our emotions to dictate our actions, it will cause utter confusion. I feel we have a pretty decent understanding of the love that exist between friends or philos. I would even go on to say that we have a good understanding of family love (storge) and sexual love (eros). However, the most important type of love is agape or the God kind of love. Agape is an undefeatable benevolence and unconquerable goodwill that always seeks the highest good of the other person, no matter what he or she does (Hayford 1452). It is self giving, not self seeking; it is unconditional, not conditional. Agape says, "What can I give?" Eros says, "What can I get?"

"For when we were still without strength, in due time
Christ died for the ungodly. For scarcely for a righteous
man will one die; yet perhaps for a good man someone

would even dare to die. But God demonstrates His own
love toward us, in that while we were yet still sinners,
Christ died for us," (Rom. 5:6-8).

Could you imagine what it would be like to die for someone
who hated the very ground you walked on? Could you imagine
being beaten to death for someone whose life totally
contradicted everything you stood for? Could you fathom being
crucified under false pretenses in order to have the weight of
sin, sickness, disease and death dropped upon your shoulders
and still be rejected? Do you not realize that God loved you
before you had the ability to love yourself? He loved you when
the world considered you to be unlovable. He looked beyond
your faults and saw your need. He realized your condition
was not your conclusion, because He knew the greatness
which lied dormant on the inside of you.

My Concept of Love

I have already described how my relationship with my father
directly affected my dating relationships. I had accepted and
was content with the presence of counterfeit love because I had
no idea of what the real thing was. I knew there was something
more than what I was receiving. What I did not know is that God
was what I was yearning for. As a result, I tried to fulfill a spiritual
desire by carnal means. I found myself becoming a bank headed
for bankruptcy because I had allowed people to withdraw funds
from my account without ever having the intentions of making a
deposit. When you make continuous withdrawals from a natural
bank account and never deposit any funds, a negative balance
is the result. My mental and emotional well being had been
stripped to the point where I didn't love myself. And since I
could not love myself, loving someone else, in my own strength
was impossible. But, thank God for Jesus! He is the lover of my
soul and because of Him, I know what love is. I don't have to

accept the presence of a counterfeit lover in my life because I have the real thing, which is Jesus!

How do you go from having a casual acquaintance with God to an intimate relationship with Him? Fasting, praying, reading and studying the Word of God are all important when you desire to become closer to God. However, praise and worship is instrumental in developing a true love relationship with the Lord. As stated before, when we give God praise, we thank and commend Him for what He has done for us. But, when we worship God it means to stoop or bow down before Him in reference in an act of submission. It is an intimate spiritual encounter. In worship, we invite God to come on the inside of us and take up residence. When we allow God to pitch a tent in us, He is then able to fill voids, pierce stony hearts, heal emotional and mental scars and wash away the residue from our past. God inhabits or lives in our praises, but when we worship Him, He comes and takes us where He lives and gives us an understanding of who He is. It is then we understand the true aspect of love.

God desires to make a permanent residence within you; however, He cannot come in if He sees a sign in your spirit marked occupied. He wants to teach you agape so that philos, storge and eros can be placed in their proper perspective. He wants to fill all your voids and pierce the heart made hard by circumstance. He desires to heal all of your emotional and mental scars and wash away all the residue of those things you try to hide. Will you allow Him to come in?

Food for Thought

When we decide to allow God to show us what love is, we must be careful not to bring our carnal ideas into our relationship with God. This is very difficult, since most of our ideas about love were based outside of God. Nevertheless, since there is nothing that is too hard for God, this is only a minor detail. God knew how much work needed to be done in us when He called us. So just sit back and watch God move!

Questions to Ponder

1. Do I really know what love is? Explain.

_____
_____
_____
_____
_____
_____

2. Where did my first concept of love originate?

_____
_____
_____
_____
_____
_____

3. Which type of love can I relate the most to: Agape, Eros, Philos or Storge? Why?

_____
_____
_____
_____
_____
_____

Chapter Twenty Two

This Flesh, This Flesh

"But put on the Lord Jesus Christ, and make no
provisions for the flesh, to fulfill its lusts,"
(Rom. 13:14).

I know this is a topic that everybody can relate to, to some
degree. All of us have had to decide whether or not to give in to
the desires of our flesh. Whether you are a virgin or not you have
had to address the topic of sex. So, even if you are a virgin, if you
have kissed passionately, hugged closely or groped, you've
experienced giving in to a desire initiated by the feelings of your
flesh. So don't try to go innocent on me.

As mentioned earlier, many of our ideas about dating were
instituted while we were yet unsaved. Since we live in such a
sexually promiscuous society, premarital sex is quite common.
Because so many single Christians have been sexually active
before marriage, many have no idea of what Christian dating is
about, or even if such a thing exists. That is why I am so elated I
will be able to give my husband something no man can claim
he's had. While this is very admirable, it has been an extremely
difficult road to travel; and through my interesting expeditions,
I've come across many speed bumps and road blocks. Sexual
frustrations plague me several times a month and I sometimes
want to give in to my flesh. However, after I take a chill pill and

a shower, I conclude sex is not worth the time I have spent growing closer to God and getting more intimate with Him.

At any rate, I know what troubles lie in the flesh. Flesh does not only mean "The inability to keep raging hormones under control". Would you like to know what the word 'flesh' really means?

Fulfilling + Lust + Edifying + Selfish + Hungers = Flesh

The flesh is self-seeking, for it will hurt others in order to be gratified. The flesh is almost always associated with sex however, this is not always the case. If you, at anytime have done something to please yourself without considering others, you have fulfilled the desire of your flesh. Every time God told you to do one thing, but you decided to do another, you were pleasing your flesh. Look at how Paul describes it.

> "For what I am doing, I do not understand. For what I will to do, that I do not practice, but what I hate I do. For I know that in me (that is, in my flesh) nothing good dwells; for to will is present with me, but how to perform what is good I do not find," (Rom. 7:15 & 18).

For the most part, sin is pleasing to the flesh. However, it separates man from God. That is why the flesh and the spirit are constantly warring with one another. The winner is determined by the one who contains the greater strength. The one you feed the most will reign as champion in your life. So I ask you, what have you eaten lately? Did you feed your spirit the Word or submit to a fast? If we desire to be the saved, sanctified and satisfied individuals God desires us to become, we must decide which appetite we are going to feed and which one we are going to starve and let die.

Let me dispel a lie. Just because we are saved and sanctified does not mean our hormones will play a disappearing act. There is nothing wrong with having feelings; we were made to have them. Sin is only conceived when we act or give in to our raging hormones. The devil loves to remind us of who we use to be and what we use to do. He majors in his-story. So I encourage you to remind the devil of his future every time he attempts to remind you of your past. What you have done has nothing to do with who you are now in Christ. That is why we should not be afraid of sharing our testimonies because they do not define who we are currently. Testimonies are merely those past moments of test where God showed Himself strong in our lives. A testimony is the result of going through a test and coming out with a passing grade. So what reason do you have to be ashamed of what you've endured and reigned as champion over? Do not allow the devil to whisper bitter nothings into your spirit. Neither allow him to trick you into acting upon your impulses. His purpose is to steal, kill and destroy you. Don't let him win!

I would love to tell you that prayer and supplication will stop your being horny, but it is not so, I know because I have tried it. When your body has experienced being aroused and then it suddenly goes 'cold turkey', it begins to react. That is one of the penalties you pay for having sexual relationships outside of marriage. While it is natural for these feelings to exist, do not give in to temptation. The best thing to do is to keep yourself out of the kitchen and then you will have not have to worry about the fire burning you. In other words, intimate kissing and petting is not wise. No, it's not sex, but your flesh is being indulged and it can produce the same results, when done correctly! So, if you have to lie in a tub of ice to stay holy, then do it. By any means necessary, stay holy. Meanwhile, pray and ask God to help you await the arrival of your due time. Wait on Him to give you who He has destined you to have. Don't marry someone just because you think they would be good in bed or because you have tested their waters. Once you are married, you won't spend your entire marriage between the sheets. Fornicating is not the answer, so do not give in to an orgasm. It doesn't take a long time to make sex good if the two parties are willing to explore and be creative. However, it takes a lifetime to create the attributes necessary for a successful marriage.

A Means of Escape

> "No temptation has overtaken you except such as
> is common to man; but God is faithful, who will not
> allow you to be tempted beyond what you are able,
> but with temptation will also make the way of escape,
> that you may be able to bear it," (I Cor. 10:13).

Temptation involves being persuaded to take a wrong course of action. It involves the remote possibility of sinning. Sin only takes place when we yield to temptation. God will always provide the way of escape; we must decide whether we will take the way of escape He has made for us. I can remember in times past, I would get myself into these compromising sexual situations and I would hear the Holy Ghost urging me to stop, but I was more concerned with gratifying my flesh and enjoying the moment. Even when I surrendered my all to God, I was still very ignorant as to what holy living was really about. I did not know anything about relationship, just religion. I was very unlearned when it came to having a personal relationship with the Lord. Until a few years ago, I did not know how essential a prayer life was; I didn't realize the power that lies in praise. I also didn't know the difference between praise and worship. As you can see, all of my "I did not knows'" originated from the fact that I did not read my Bible.

It is critical that we read and meditate on the Word for ourselves. Without meditation there can be no revelation. Do not wait for your pastor or bishop to tell you to read your Sword. God wants to commune with you individually. Going to church is fine, singing in the choir is fine and listening to people minister is fine. But, if you don't know the Word for yourself, how will you be able to distinguish between false and sound doctrine? Your temple must contain substance; the Bible provides the steady diet we need to be sustained.

Dating As A Christian Woman

We have already determined that being led by the flesh will do more harm and no good. With this in mind, how should a woman of God date? I'm glad you asked! We have already determined that the majority of our ideals about love and relationships were formed outside of our relationship with God. With this in mind, most of us accepted the Lord into our lives after having some type of carnal experience or after conversion, gave into sin's enticement. Whatever the case may be, many of us do not know how to date without using the world's methods.

Being a woman of God is a privilege and an honor. In addition, being a woman called into ministry is something not to be taken lightly or for granted. Now, when I refer to being called into ministry, I do not mean preaching and teaching only. If you sing with the anointing of God on every note, you are in ministry. If you work in the nursery, answer the prayer lines or usher with grace, you are in ministry. At any rate, in times past, women have not filled many leadership positions in the Body of Christ mainly due to the bondage's of tradition. This distorted view of women in ministry is sometimes supported by using the following Scripture: "And I do not permit a woman to teach or have authority over a man, but to be in silence," (I Tim. 2:12). I do not believe Paul was stating that a woman should not be in ministry. The point to stress here is the woman was made to be a helpmate to the man; she should never try to become domineering in her position. The Bible gives many accounts of women who were active in the ministry. The Prophet Joel prophesied that God said He would, "Pour out My Spirit on all flesh; your sons and your daughters shall prophesy." Surely, God would never come short of fulfilling His word.

Dating as a woman of God is a very explosive topic to discuss. First, dating from the Christian perspective is unique because we are not governed by the world's standards. In addition, anyone who calls themselves a Christian should have their steps ordered when it comes to dating because their every move will be scrutinized. As ministers of reconciliation, we must realize some people wait in the wings for our failure. We cannot give the devil any leverage to hang us by using our own rope. There are a few general principles I feel are crucial for a woman of God to consider when dating.

1. Your relationship with God is first; your call to ministry is second.
2. Allow the Lord to choose your mate.
3. A boyfriend/spouse is not a substitute for but an addition to you.
4. Do not allow your good to be evil spoken of.

For those of you who are already working in ministry, it is easy to get caught up in the work of ministry and forget whom the work is being done for. Keep your motives pure. Next, I do not believe a Christian should have to date the nation to come into contact with their mate. We should focus on delighting ourselves in the Lord and in turn our desires will be filled. In essence, let God be God! Thirdly, a perspective companion cannot fill any voids that may exist in our lives. We should work to have all past hurts and issues dealt with before entering into a new relationship. The last thing you want to do is bring mental suitcases or emotional garment bags from an old relationship into a new one. Lastly, how you date is based on your individual integrity. If the Holy Ghost is alive and well within you, He will lead and guide you into all truth. Allow Him to give you your list of do's and don'ts.

Coming into contact with the person we will spend the rest of our lives with is not a subject to be taken lightly. The most important aspect to remember out of everything that has been said is to let God be God. Don't move according to the flesh because we know that no good thing dwells there. What God has for you is for you; and when the time comes He will reveal your man of purpose to you!

Food for Thought

A male friend of mine brought something to my attention, which bears repeating. Sometimes, we as Christian women can be very aggressive in our pursuit of a Godly man. I know the choices can seem quite slim at times, but the truth is if you desire to be married, God has a mate for you. Stop eyeing the alter and choir for prospects. Just because a man is saved it does not make him qualified to be your husband; it only makes him eligible. I must admit, I once began to pursue a man I had an interest in a little aggressively until the Lord told me to "Let him watch you glean." After I walked in obedience to what God said, He was attracted to the God he saw in me, not my shape. Though physical attraction is important, it is not good enough to make a relationship last. Don't only go for what the natural eye perceives but for what the spirit can receive.

Questions to Ponder

1. Do I find myself feeding my spirit more than my flesh or my flesh more than my spirit? Explain.

_____

_____

_____

_____

_____

2. At this point in my life, do I feel I am ready for marriage? Explain.

_____

_____

_____

_____

_____

3. Do I consider marriage to be a ministry? Why or why not? If so, am I prepared to minister to the man or woman God has prepared for me?

_____

_____

_____

_____

_____

_____

Chapter Twenty Three

Patience Is The Essence

"By your patience possess your souls,"
(Luke 21:19).

Patience is truly a virtue that is not groomed overnight. If you have been through a lot, you know that it is your tribulations which produces endurance or patience, read Romans 5:3-4. We must decide that we want God to take complete control of every area of our lives. In doing this, we place everything into His hands and out of ours. The way God does things will not be the way we think things should have been done. But God knows the end result; we can only wonder until He decides to reveal it to us.

"For my thoughts are not your thoughts; nor are your
ways my ways', says the Lord. 'For as the heavens are
higher than the earth, so are my ways higher than your
ways, and my thoughts your thoughts," (Isa. 55:8-9).

See, we can't even attempt to think like God or conceive His thoughts. So why do we foolishly attempt to master mind some ridiculous scheme when we say that He is in complete control of our lives?

As I mentioned before, I have had four relationships that I would consider to have been serious. Each one of these young men had similar characteristics, but they were all quite unique.

I found myself trying to fit all the men in my life into an image of what I thought I wanted. And to be honest, I didn't consult God on anyone I dated except for the last relationship I had. I thought I needed to play someone's mother and adjust myself and sacrifice my needs and desires to please the other party. Sometimes God will allow certain people to come into our lives to grow us and to make spiritual deposits into our lives. Unfortunately, we can misconstrue a spiritual concern that a person may have for us as an emotional attachment. I have seen this happen time and time again and have actually been a victim of it myself.

I have never had a problem with commitment. However, I think my motives for wanting to be committed were misguided. At one point in my life I was tired of seeing all of my friends getting married in front of my face. I was an easy target for being hurt because I would give my heart to any man who blew in my ear, and that is not an exaggeration! In my mind, I thought I could make him love me or do enough to make him want to stay. Even though it took a few years, I realized that I could not make a man stay where he did not want to be.

"Commit your way to the Lord; Trust also in Him,
and He shall bring it to past," (Ps. 37:5).

"But those who wait on the Lord shall renew their
strength. They shall mount up on wings like eagles.
They shall run and not be weary, They shall walk
and not faint," (Isa. 40:31).

"But first seek the kingdom of God and His
righteousness, and all these things shall be
added to you," (Matt. 6:33).

These Scriptures admonish us to possess something our flesh wars against, patience. The first Scripture talks about committing our ways to the Lord. Sometimes we find it easier to commit to everyone and everything but our relationship with the lord. God could do so much for us if we would only place our entire lives into His hands. Trust the Lord, stand on the promises of His Word, have faith in what He has told you. If God has spoken it, then it shall come to pass. Also, we should give God the impossible situations to handle, without putting our hands in it and possibly producing "Ishamael's". When we do not see in the natural what God has promised and still believe in what He has said, our faith moves Him into action. Having pity parties, faithlessness, walking in defeat and doubt does not move God. A lifestyle of faith does! If we make serving God our priority, then and only then will we inherit all those things He has promised us.

In this technological society we live in, it is not abnormal to not like to wait. We can cook an entire meal in the microwave in twenty minutes. We can fax a letter and have information in our hands from across the world in a matter of seconds. So why should be have to wait for God to send us a mate? Well, as we have already discovered, God does not operate on the time schedule in which we live. He is not limited to space and He is not obligated by time. God has so much in store for us as single men and women. He has already called so many of us to be teachers and preachers of the Gospel, and so much more. It is up to you to seek God for your individual purpose. Our lives as singles should be focused on what God has called us to do and be today, not a year from now! The mate will come, the marriage will take place and many seeds will be produced! Just be patient!

Being saved, sanctified and satisfied does not mean we will forget we are men or women. In addition, it does not mean we will no longer desire companionship, kisses and hugs. It most definitely does not mean we will discontinue having adrenaline rushes and estrogen fits! What it does mean is we have realized that we have a power that is greater than what our feelings or hormones may dictate.

Experience: The Best Teacher (Sometimes!)

At this point in my writing this book, I am proofreading and preparing to send this book to a publishing company. While doing this, the Holy Spirit reminded me that I hadn't discussed any of my previous relationships. I guess subconsciously I thought I could get by without being too personal. For the most part, I am a private person and I don't allow many people to get into my personal space. However, I realize that some healing needs to take place in me by ministering to you. Even though I mentioned I have been involved in four different relationships, I only want to discuss the two which have made the deepest impact upon and in me.

Love Overboard

At the beginning of my high school years, I experienced the disappointment of puppy love with a guy named Brian. He had made it clear that he did not want to be involved with someone who was as boring as I was. After being with him, my self esteem was at an all time low. I found myself desiring to be loved by somebody, anybody! At the time, the relationship I had with my mom wasn't good and my siblings were much older than I, so I didn't feel they could relate to me. Enter Kenneth Shaw.

When I met Kenneth, initially I was not attracted to him, looks wise. We met while singing in a community choir and later we participated in a church play being directed by his girlfriend at the time. For some reason, he kept coming around me and would sometimes lay his head on my shoulder, as if he found a place of rest in me. We exchanged phone numbers and began to talk occasionally. Kenneth had a dynamic personality. He was fun and he made me feel like I was important, which was something I had not experienced with the men in my life. Nevertheless, there was one situation at hand: He still had a girlfriend. At any rate, we continued to talk over the next few months and then it dwindled. I thought that was the end until . . .

About two years later, I left Jacksonville Florida to go to college at FAMU in Tallahassee Florida. While on campus during new student orientation, I ran into Kenneth who said he was going to attend the local community college. Later I found out he was lying and was leeching off of someone who he called a friend and had never intended on going to college at that time.

While in school, I began to attend Watson Temple Church of God in Christ (C.O.G.I.C.). Though it wasn't like my home church, the teaching and order of service was what I was familiar with. Besides, I felt the Lord was leading me to become a part of this fellowship, so I did. About a year later, I answered God's call for me into the ministry. I was so scared, until it was six months before I talked to my pastor about what God was speaking to me. He was such an awesome pastor and such a man of God and a person of integrity. I had heard that if he didn't feel as if God had called you, he would tell you to go back and pray. This didn't deter me from my purpose because I knew it was God; I was in no way trying to call myself. After talking to him, he informed me that he wanted me to be prepared to do my initial sermon in a few weeks. The anointing of God really flowed and for the first time in my life I knew I was where God wanted me to be.

Over the course of the next five months, I ran into Kenneth while at a district and national C.O.G.I.C. convention. At our first meeting, I really didn't give him much thought. He gave me his phone number but I didn't follow up with a phone call. The second time I saw him I questioned whether this could be God showing me who my husband was. At no time did I question whether this could be an "angel of light"; oh no, this could not be the devil, could it?

" . . . For Satan himself transforms himself into an
angel of light," (II Cor. 11:14).

One thing about Satan, he is easily recognizable as a roaring lion and as a serpent, but not so easily seen as an angel of light. Make no mistake about it, the adversary is no fool. He has strategically designed ways to take us off course. He will not use those things in which we have overcome; he will only use those areas in which we are still weak. Even though I was focused on ministry and finishing my degree in English, I still was longing for the attention of a man. This was my point of weakness.

As a result of our second meeting, I called Kenneth. During our first conversation he told me about how much he had changed and that he was not the same person I once knew. Foolishly, I fell for the drama he was starring in. If a person has to tell you that they have changed and they can't show you with actions, the person really hasn't changed. I didn't realize how caught up in the idol of companionship I was. I had witnessed my friends get married and have children before I even obtained a steady relationship. This is so disheartening until we as women will accept the first man who seems half-way decent. I know it is difficult to deal with loneliness and to want to be held and kissed, but there is not one there to turn to. As a woman, it is natural to feel these things. However, as women of God we have the ability to have control over these feelings and not have them control us.

Over the next three months or so I was told how beautiful and precious I was. I had never even looked at myself as being pretty or beautiful. When you have to have someone else affirm who you are, you will never come to the point where you believe it yourself. If no one else tells you how pretty you are, it should be O.K. because you have already told yourself. Self-esteem has nothing to do with how other people see you, it is how you view yourself. What happens is since a person may view themselves with such a low concept, the individual looks to the praise and accolades of others to tell them who they are. As a result of never being complemented from men, the image I had of myself was quite low. Now, don't think I was never told I was pretty because I was. However, the compliments normally came from women or men who were not interested in me romantically. There is a difference!

One day I received a letter drenched in cologne from Kenneth telling me he didn't want to talk to me anymore. He went on to say that he wasn't ready to be in a relationship because he needed to be more focused on God. I had no gripes with that. My confusion came as a result of me not being the one who had initiated any relationship talks. I didn't ask him to marry me, he asked me! (I declined, thank you Jesus!) Being that as it may, I complied. I didn't write, call or contact him. If he wanted to focus on God, I was going to let him focus. About a month after receiving the letter, I went home for the wedding of an acquaintance. While there, I ran into Kenneth again. We talked and went out after the wedding. I allowed him to take me home and keep my car until the next morning because I didn't feel like taking him home across town. We hadn't decided to resume what we had started; we were just going to let things be.

Kenneth called me around 8:45 a.m. the next morning (Sunday) to let me know that he was on his way to get me for church. Time kept passing and he never showed. About an hour or so later, I received a call requesting me to come pick up my car from the police. I was then given the location of my vehicle; I hung up the phone in mass confusion praying that Kenneth was O.K. As I begin to walk out of my driveway, a strange van pulled up. It was Tiffany and her brother who had come to take me to my car. Later, I found out that they had seen my car parked in the middle of the street in front of a police car. On the way, Tiffany asked if I knew that Kenneth did not have a license. I said, "What? Do you think I would allow someone to drive my car without a license to do so?" I was so mad until I could have spit bullets. When I arrived, Kenneth' cousin was sitting on the passenger side of my car and he was in the back of the police car. One of the officers checked my license to make sure I was the owner of the vehicle. After that I was told that Kenneth was going to jail for charges unknown to me. I had no desire at all to see him. I knew he had been involved in illegal activity before, but I thought that portion of his life was over. I felt so betrayed.

The next day I decided to call to the police station to find out what the charges were. I discovered that he had been charged with violation of probation and grand theft (auto). Later on that week, I decided to pay him a visit in order to get some answers. To make a long story short, I decided to keep in contact with him because I didn't want to kick him while he was down. Over the course of his four month incarceration, he sent me romantic letters and he thanked me for being in his life. He made me all of these wonderful promises of relationship bliss once he was released. I felt compelled to stay with him because I was sure God had placed me in his life to get him where he needed to be. What I didn't realize is Kenneth was playing on my vulnerability. He no more wanted a relationship with me than he wanted a free trip to hell! Ladies, a man in prison or jail will promise you anything to get you where they want you. They are incarcerated 24 hours a day, 7 days a week. All they have time to do is think and plot.

Once he was released from jail, he came to stay with me at my apartment in Tallahassee for a week. What a huge mistake! Lord, I am so glad that I did not have sex with him; and believe me, it wasn't because I didn't want to. I tried to give my virginity away but somehow he had viewed that "Off Limits" sign God had placed on me. We had some too close for comfort situations, but penetration never took place. And I thank God for it! Now, I don't feel like I have missed anything. Believe me, when I marry the man God has ordained me to spend the rest of my life with, there will be plenty of time to play make up!

On the trip back to Jacksonville, he started to tell me things about himself I wasn't aware of. He told me of his involvement with selling drugs, being stabbed, shot at, grazed by a bullet, and being involved in gangs. We also talked about the non existent relationship he had with his father and family. Because of his track record, his family expected him to fail. As a result, I took it upon myself to become his support system and be what others had failed to. Unfortunately, I did not realize that you can't fulfill a position in someone's life if they don't want you there. I found myself telling him "There is nothing you can do to change the way I feel about you." Though these words were meant to encourage and strengthen him, they ended up destroying me emotionally.

Over the next few months, I heard from Kenneth less and

less. After I graduated from college in December of 1997, I moved back to Jacksonville. Sometime in January, Kenneth located me and started calling again. At this time, I didn't know he was living with a young lady named Keeva who was carrying his baby. A month or so later she had an abortion while he was out of town. I know this crushed him because he had always told me of how much he wanted children. Eventually, he broke off the relationship because she was cheating on him with someone else. Kenneth was finally getting a taste of how being deceitful and cunning felt. I had also been informed by a relative of mine who worked with him, that he was showing the poems and letters I wrote to him to the people he worked with. How immature? In addition, I was told that he had said some negative things about my appearance. Even after all of this, I still found myself being like the father was with his wayward son (Luke 15:11-32): In spite of all of the events which had transpired, I found myself facing him with my arms stretched wide open as Kenneth came running.

Though I didn't realize it then, I had become a place of refuge for Kenneth. He knew he could always come back to me no matter what the circumstances were. In me he found acceptance, unconditional love and a peace he had never received. However, there was a period I went through where I would attempt to say and do things to make him hurt the way he had hurt me. What I failed to see then is that he would never hurt the way I'd been hurt. I'm not saying that they don't hurt, because that is not true. However, men tend to hurt hard but not long; we hurt long and hard.

When God had instructed me to attend World Harvest Bible College I was both excited and fearful. I had never been almost 1,000 miles from what was familiar to me before. This was truly a faith move for me. I knew if I followed God, I could not be steered wrong. Kenneth took me out to lunch before I left town. We were not together at this time. He told me of the regret he had concerning us and that he was sorry for what he had put me through. Once I left, I had every intention on leaving Kenneth and the memories of what we had behind. Little did I know that there were many issues between us that needed to be resolved. It wasn't until later that I realized open wounds bleed and become infected; they don't disappear!

A New Chapter Begins

When I arrived in Columbus Ohio, I was so pumped! I couldn't believe that God had afforded me the opportunity to be under such an anointed ministry and man of God (Pastor Rod Parsley). I went there with my focus being on Jesus and the call He had placed upon my life. I wanted to get all I could, while I could. I was so sure that God had called me to be an evangelist. I could see myself going from city to city doing spiritual drive-bys on people. Unexpectantly, the Holy Spirit told me to change my major from evangelism to pastoral studies. This interrupted what I thought my purpose was for being at bible college. This event is what initialized my periods of breaking.

So many times we can think that we know what God has destined us to be. What we do not realize is that so many times our actions are flesh led and not God led. God had to take me across five state lines, away from my family so that I could lose myself. Flesh has no place in the ministry or in a relationship with God. I realized that I needed to lose my agenda and gain God's agenda. I spent the next few months being pressed, pruned and pricked by the Lord. And to be honest, I am still being pressed, pruned and pricked. In order for our motives to remain pure, we must go through purification.

While at Bible College, I met Jackson. He was extremely nice and very handsome. He too had an awesome personality and above all I could tell that he really loved God. I initially began to pursue him a little carnally. After being convicted by the Holy Spirit, I ceased my pursuit. I was instructed to "Let him watch you glean". After this, I stopped chasing after him; I was determined to let Boaz find Ruth. I was tired of closed-ended relationships. Surely, I deserved much better than what I had received in the past.

During the latter part of my first semester, Kenneth called again. The persistence of this man was phenomenal. He started to feed me the same old lies of the past; you know, how much he was in love with me and wanted to be with me. It is so strange to me how his so-called love for me could not keep him out of another woman's bed. When I went home for Christmas break and saw him, he acted as if he didn't have time for me. How contradictory, but this was so Kenneth!

In the meantime, Jackson and I were getting closer. We talked a few time during Christmas break and we had some awesome conversations. He was so easy to talk to and he never told me what I wanted to hear, but always what I needed to hear. Right before school ended for the semester, he confided in me about something he was dealing with. From that trust was birthed. Ladies, one thing men desire is a woman they can trust. They have so many demands on them as is, not including the task of being a man of God. If a man knows he can trust you with his insecurities and fears without worrying about them being disclosed, he knows he has struck gold or better yet a diamond!

Both of us had similar goals and we had a lot in common. We got along great and in January of 2000, we decided to make things official. It seemed to be the perfect set up; his family loved me, especially his mom, his friends and church family were also cool with me. Things were progressing in the right direction until . . .

In April of the same year, he decided that we should separate for a while. This hit me hard because I just knew without a shadow of a doubt that Jackson was to be my husband. I did not understand what was going on. Nevertheless, we separated and only talked occasionally. We had already planned to go to Cincinnati Ohio so that he could meet a portion of my family who would be there for the weekend. Everyone loved Jackson and he loved my family too, especially my brother.

Over the course of the next month, Jackson and I continued to talk. We had also previously planned to attend my family reunion at the end of June, before we discontinued our relationship temporarily. Two weeks prior to the family reunion, my grandmother died. This was very difficult for me especially since I was so far away from home. Jackson and my roommate at the time helped me through this time. I found it hard to have a happy birthday while viewing my grandmother's body. I spent about ten years of my life living with her; she was like another mother to me. We would play Uno, guess wheel of fortune puzzles and play Jeopardy together. You never realize how important someone is to you until they are gone forever.

While home for my grandmother's home going, I ran into Kenneth at the movie theater. I tell you, the counterfeit will always keep showing up to take your focus off of the real! Anyway, he said he had been thinking about me and had mailed me a letter. I told him I would be back in town in a few weeks, but I would not be coming alone. Seeing him at that time did awake some emotions, but I just placed them under the carpet as usual. One thing about sweeping things under the carpet, it forms lumps and bumps to trip us up. That is what happens when we as women don't deal with those past painful issues. We don't need an emotional broom; we need a spiritual vacuum cleaner!

On the drive to Florida for vacation, I told Jackson that we may run into Kenneth. I had no intentions on calling or meeting him. But because we knew some of the same people and are involved with some of the same churches, our paths crossing was inevitable. Well, during our last night in Jacksonville, we saw Kenneth at a live recording concert. I introduced Jackson to Kenneth; this was somewhat awkward and I know Kenneth was caught off guard. He had never seen me with anybody other than him and for the first time he realized that I was no longer available. That night I realized that there were a lot of unsettled issues between Kenneth and I. I knew that if I wanted to give my all to Jackson, I had to loose the Kenneth ties. I was not going to mess up what God had given me with Jackson for the unstableness of Kenneth.

Once I returned to Columbus, I felt like I was going through a transition. A week later God told me that it was time to finish the book He had instructed me to start back in 1996. In addition, He told me to completely separate from Jackson so that my focus could be on Him. That was so difficult for me because our relationship was so unstable at the time and I was sure that I was going to lose him. He told me not to worry because he was not going anywhere. While on vacation he had told me that God had spoken to him and told him that I was his wife. I breathed a sigh of relief because this was only a confirmation to what God had spoken to me. Nevertheless, the Lord told me not to say anything because He was working in and on him. Ladies, if God has told you who your husband is, He will confirm what He has said through the man! When we speak prematurely, it is possible that the baby can be destroyed while in its embryonic state. So in essence, let the man be the man!

During the next month, I worked steadily on this book. In the meantime, Kenneth started calling me again. He acted as if he had a sincere interest about my well being. It didn't phase him that I was in love with another man. He was just happy that he could talk to me. He had always told me that he could get any woman he wanted if he was persistent enough. To him, I was just a welcomed challenge. Since I couldn't talk to Jackson, I made a substitution. Later, the Lord allowed me to realize that I was placing my relationship with Jackson in jeopardy. I was behooved to cut the cord forever!

I informed Kenneth that though I still cared about him, I was no longer in love with him. Him in my life only confused my emotions and made me think that I still loved him. Contrary to popular belief, you cannot love two men romantically at the same time. If you can't distinguish, I would question whether a person loves either. It takes more than enough energy to love one person the right way. Though we are awesome men and women, God didn't endow us with enough stamina to love two men or women the way He has designed us to. Once I let him know where I was coming from, he said O.K. and hung up the phone.

About a week later, I saw Jackson for the first time in seven weeks. He looked really good! Shammah! Absence truly makes the heart grow fonder. The time had come for us to endure our last year of Bible College. We had endured some very rough spots in our relationship during the past year. We figured that God has some things for us to do in ministry together. The reason I had to change my major to pastoral studies is because God is grooming me to be in ministry alongside my spouse and to minister specifically to hurting and abused women. And guess who is called to be a pastor? Yes, that's right, Jackson!

I love our relationship; it is so God! We promised from the beginning to not let the flesh dictate our relationship. We are so driven to let this be a God thing not a Jackson or Ivy thing. People have tried to push us into marriage, but we are dead set on God being the head of our union, not people. When it is time, we will both know it! In the meantime, we just continue to grow closer to each other in God because we desire to be that three-fold cord that is not easily broken. I'm glad that God has given me someone who prays for me and cares about my spiritual and physical needs (health wise). He has prayed that this book will reach nations and heal every woman who reads it. While experiencing some health issues, Jackson was right there in the ER praying and speaking words of encouragement. I do the same for him also. It is a tedious task being involved with someone who is walking out their ministry. He is a minister at his church and is constantly being tested by God and tempted by the devil. It is my responsibility to pray and intercede for him and keep a word on my tongue to minister to him. I do not find it to be a chore; this is my privilege and I fulfill the call to this ministry in honor. Marriage is a ministry; we are just laying the foundation in the dating stage. Our love has nothing to do with the flesh, because we are not going there until we are married. However, we know since we have a spiritual and an emotional tie, things can only get better from here. Glory!

Nevertheless, the presence of the counterfeit must enter again. Kenneth called again to tell me that he was engaged. I found this quite sudden since he wanted to marry me two months ago. I told him congratulations, but I thought I had made it clear that we no longer needed to communicate. He didn't take this affirmation to well. He told me, in essence, that he will never give up on what we had and that he still loved me and I was his friend forever. He said he didn't care who he was married or engaged to, he still wanted me in his life. (Sounds like fatal attraction, doesn't it?) All I could think is how in the world could I have ever been in love with someone so demanding and controlling. Prayerfully he got this message loud and clear. If not, Jackson said he would be willing to step in and talk to him.

In the midst of both of these relationships, I gained experiences that one can't grasp from a book. However, I am convinced that I don't have to experience everything to learn life's lessons. Everything monkey sees, monkey shouldn't have to do! That is why it is so important for us to share our experiences with one another. I have never been abused physically or sexually, but I have been tremendously scarred emotionally and I am sure I could teach any woman a whole lot about how to be healed, no matter how the wound was incurred. I no longer need a man to affirm me because God tells me who I am and who He is preparing me to become. When you believe what God says about you the thoughts and opinions of people are null and void!

Food for Thought

On my way back to Columbus Ohio from Florida during Christmas break in 1999, I had a connection flight in Charlotte North Carolina. Once I boarded the plane and it prepared to leave the runway, we were prohibited from leaving the runway because several planes were landing when we were scheduled to be taking off. We were where they were trying to be. Just then, the Holy Ghost said to me "a holding pattern". There are times when a plane is attempting to land, but air traffic control cannot give it the clearance it needs to land, due to weather or other situations. As a result, the plane has to circle the runway in the air until clearance can be given. Their destiny is right in view, but the time is not feasible for a safe landing. This is where some of us are spiritually. You can see what God has promised you in the spirit, but the season is not right for a "landing". Be patient, women of God, being delayed doesn't mean God has denied you! Trust me, He knows what He is doing, even when we don't have a clue!

Questions to Ponder

1. How have my life's tribulations worked patience in me?

_____

_____

_____

_____

_____

_____

2. Do I think God has me in a spiritual holding pattern. If so, how should I respond?

_____

_____

_____

_____

_____

3. Is patience a virtue I embrace or dodge? Why?

_____

_____

_____

_____

_____

Chapter Twenty Four

Being Content Where You Are

"Not that I speak in regard to need, for I have
learned in what ever state I am, to be content,"
(Phil. 4:11).

This passage of scripture gives us the key in preparing for our promise, being content where we are. If we cannot find total fulfillment in Christ, we will definitely not find it in another person. That is one reason why so many people go from relationship to relationship and bed to bed; they are looking for something that only God can give. If we continue to suffer from what I call the "I Need A Mate Syndrome", we will lower our Godly principles in order to help God in the decision making process. And make no mistake about it, if you lower your standards to get, you will have to continue to lower them to keep. We should be so satisfied in our relationship with the Lord until all other areas of our lives are fulfilled too. Please do not marry anyone to fill voids and to feel sufficient. We should lean on the everlasting arms of Jesus for safety and security. If you are not satisfied in your relationship with the Lord, please stop those wedding bells from ringing. It is best to do things God's way or no way at all.

Inner Beauty versus Outer Body

I am sure all of us have heard the saying, "Everything that

glitters isn't gold"; well, I am here to tell you, it is oh so truth. Many of us run the risk of missing out on our 'Boaz' because we want him to be 6'2, dark, with a six-pack and an anointing like Bishop T.D. Jakes! It is O.K. to desire, but let's not limit God because we cannot extend our eyes past the exterior of a person. If God were to judge us like the world and look on the outward appearance to choose His royal priesthood, many of us would not be chosen vessels.

> "Do not look at his appearance or at his physical stature, because I have refused him. For the Lord does not see as man sees; for man looks at the outward appearance, but the Lord looks at the heart," (I Sam. 16:7).

I don't know about you, but I don't want a man fine in statue, but refused by God! And likewise, we should not disregard certain men or women because they don't meet all of our abstract criteria. I believe with age comes much maturity and a coming into the knowledge of what really is important. My perspective on what I thought I needed in a husband ten years ago is not the same as what I know I need now. The characteristics I desire in a mate have nothing to do with his physique. A Georgio Armani suit, a bottle of Balderssarini cologne, a pair of Kenneth Cole shoes and a facial will fix up any man's outward appearance real nice! But I need to know, what a man can offer me. Can you carry me in the spirit? Are you able to stand in the midst of the storm outside of the presence of people? What is your vision for your life and perspective wife and children? Where do you see yourself in five or ten years? Are you in a position to provide for the needs of our family or do you even have a clue? I know some of you think this is asking too much. Fortunately, for me I realize I am worthy of a man of God and not a "busta" which is what I've had in the past. I am a woman with nations in her belly and I refused to be tied to a man with a "local" mentality.

Searching versus Waiting

Have you ever lost something valuable or precious to you? You looked all over and could not find it. You tried to back track your steps for the day and you still came up empty. You were on a search for something. On the opposite side of the spectrum, have you ever ordered something through the mail? You knew exactly what was coming, however you were not sure of when it would arrive. Even though you may have been given a certain time to expect delivery, things can happen to delay arrival. In this position, you were waiting for something which had already been promised to you.

As a woman of God, we are in the position of waiting on God to deliver what He has already promised. The key to waiting is not sitting in a corner with our legs crossed; that is being complacent. When a waiter waits on a table, he serves his customers. He does not sit down at the table next to them. With this in mind, we should be serving God with everything we have. That means with our time and with our tithe. We must do what is required if we desire God to hold up His end of the promise. However, once God gives us that promised seed, we should not become unfaithful and fall by the wayside. That is the time to take everything to a higher place so that God can take us to the next level. Increase your prayer time, your personal Bible study time, live a life of fasting and consecration. As a result, God will move for you consistently and not just occasionally.

The only people who are in search are those Christians who are being led by the will of their flesh or those who don't know Jesus at all. There is no need for us to search because our Christian walk is not equivalent to a maze. There is no need for us to search for the things of God because we know exactly where to look, in God!

The key to moving with God's flow is being content with where He has you now. Don't worry about anything else. As long as you are accomplishing those things He has designed for you to do today, you are where you are suppose to be, in the center of His will!

Food For Thought

Right before submitting this book for publishing, I decided to get some comments from single and married persons concerning relationships. For the single person, I asked them to provide me with any subjects they would like to see covered in a book geared toward singles. For the most part, I covered every area placed before me, with divine inspiration from the Holy Ghost! In addition, I asked some married individuals "What issues in a single's life do you feel need to be addressed before a person makes the decision to get married?" With that said, I received an awesome insight from one young woman's perspective and I'd like to share it with you in closing.

1. Pray and ask God to bring him/her into your life. HE knows what you need, when you need it. God can filter out the fools for you!
2. Go to Church together. Talk about God and study His Word so you can see where they are spiritually. If he/she does not have a personal relationship with God, that is an issue!
3. I would highly recommend Stormie O'Martain's book, "The Power of a Praying Wife/Husband." My husband and I were on the verge of getting a divorce, but prayer saved our marriage. I would highly recommend this book to anyone who is engaged to be married. It will save you from dealing with a lot of unnecessary drama!
4. Be sure you can talk to this person. There will be times when the sex is boring or you just don't feel like it. Cuddling and talking in bed is so romantic to me!
5. Make sure you have a friendship. Friends have the tendency of growing together and even when they argue, they are willing to forgive and go on.
6. Make sure you know about each other's past. Know about how they relate to their family, how they grew up, if they have children, "baby momma/daddy drama", finances, past relationships. All of this will play a factor in your marriage. If

you don't know about these things and the person brings baggage to the marriage, you'll have to decide if you love them enough to help them unload their baggage.

7. Specifically, know about how they were raised. Know how he/she relates to their parents, siblings and other family. If he/she takes heed to EVERYTHNG their mother/father says, take notice. If they relate to their family by yelling, screaming and arguing, beware. My husband's family are basically fools. Before I started to pray for his relationship with them, when he was around them he was a totally different person. Thank God for change!

8. Do not get involved intimately before the marriage. This complicates things for women because we put our emotions into lovemaking. As a Christian, you don't want to allow just anyone's spirit to join with yours.

9. Watch how that person handles stress or difficult situations. Do not allow anyone to put their hands on you. If he/she is physically abusive, a marriage will not change them.

10. Lastly, know their financial status before you marry! If a person has bad credit, you will need to know this before you apply for a house and/or car or other things.

WB,
Dallas, Texas

Questions to Ponder

1. For me as an individual, what are the keys to me being content with where I am today?

   _____

   _____

   _____

   _____

   _____

   _____

2. Regarding a mate, is my focus more on inner beauty or outer body? Explain.

   _____

   _____

   _____

   _____

   _____

   _____

3. Do I find myself searching or waiting? Explain.

   _____

   _____

   _____

   _____

   _____

   _____

Epilogue

"Love Under New Management"

It is so easy to believe God when everything in your life is going smoothly. God is good when the rent is paid and He is worthy to be praised when our bodies are well. However, is God still good when you have to rob Peter to pay Paul? Is He still praise worthy when your body has been afflicted with pain and your condition is absent of a diagnosis? Sure He is!

My life has taken many strange loops and turns since I began writing this book. The Apostle Paul records these words in I Corinthians 9:27:

"But I discipline my body and bring it into subjection,
lest, when I have preached to others, I myself should
become disqualified."

In essence, no person is fit to be used of God unless they have surrendered their total being to Him. Whenever you tell someone about Jesus, whether it be through witnessing to one or in a crowd of thousands, you are responsible for every word you utter from your lips. With this in mind, I have always tried to represent God by living a holy life before Him and those I come into contact with on a daily basis. I never want someone to look at my life and not see who I say I represent. I truly believe that the best witness is the life I live and not the words I say.

If this book does not speak to anyone else, though I know it will, it has spoken to me. I realize the entire key to being **Saved, Sanctified, Satisfied** and **Single** lies in my ability to trust God. I know it sounds simple, but ask yourself, "Do I really trust God?" Before you say yes, ponder for a few minutes. I am learning everyday how to trust and rely on God for every part of my life. For instance, if I was doing such a great job in my selection of men, why would I need to wait on God to choose my mate? Just think, If we really believed God is who He says He is, would we doubt or second guess the plans He has for us so much?

When God spoke to me and told me Jackson was my husband, it was signed, sealed and delivered for me. I did not need to go and tell Jackson what God had said because I knew God would eventually speak those same words to him, and he did. In addition, I did not need to get a hundred and one confirmations to assure me that the voice I heard was God's; when you have the Confirmer living on the inside of you, you do not need to seek a confirmation.

Once I came into right standing with God, I grasped a firm handle as to what love really was or is. I realized the same type of selfless love Jesus exhibited when he died on the Cross is the same love I needed to demonstrate in all of my relationships. God has given me the awesome ability to love people in spite of themselves because this is the same love He has shown to me.

With this in mind, I have always desired to be loved with the same intensity in which I love. My desire to be married is not based on a yearning to fulfill a plethora of carnal appetites. It would be my pleasure to have the opportunity to minister to God's chosen man for me in every aspect, whether it be mentally, emotionally, spiritually or physically. Of course I had specific characteristics and attributes I desired, but I refused to allow my will to override God's plan for me.

When Jackson's path crossed mine, I knew God's hand was in place. We were so much in sync with one another. At the onset of our relationship, we vowed not to allow the flesh to take control, and we kept that vow. We prayed for and encouraged one another on a consistent basis; there was a measure of trust between us which insured an infallible foundation. We openly communicated about any and every thing. We accepted the occurrences that transpired in the other's past and promised to keep these events private. Jackson was already operating in ministry so I found life in hearing him preach God's Word. I took pleasure in interceding for him and building him up. He was "My Priest" and I was his Diamond, surely nothing could prohibit this union from taking place, right?

Unfortunately, somewhere within a two-year period, Jackson decided that fulfilling the desires of his flesh was more important than having God's will being done in his life. He exclaimed that since I was not physically what he had asked God for he did not desire to marry me. I could not believe our two year God ordained relationship had been abruptly discontinued because of some superficial, physical attributes which should not have been important or vital to the survival of a successful relationship. My height never seemed to be an issue when I turned my plate down to pray for God's anointing to show up whenever he was to preach. My figure was not a concern while I was weeping, wailing and going into enemy hell territory to combat attacks against him regarding his personal struggles. Whenever he needed prayer, my phone was ringing off the hook. Whenever he needed an ear of concern or an honest opinion, it was my ear and opinion he longed for because he knew God would be in it. So I wondered, what was the real reason?

I almost drove myself into a state of insanity, trying to figure out what went wrong. I only came to one conclusion: You cannot make someone obey God if they have chosen their will as more important. I experienced so many different emotions until I cannot even begin to describe them all to you. I had to pray and ask God to help me with this because some strong dislike and even hate began to come into my heart. But, you know what? God is still good and in control! He is not the one who has disappointed me; it was man who failed to do what God had instituted.

Though my soul has been afflicted with many wounds, my spirit is being renewed day by day. God is healing me day by day; the last thing I want to do is blame the next man for what the last man has done. I believe there are some true men of God who place the will of God before their own. And as I continue to focus on being **Saved, Sanctified, Satisfied** and **Single,** one of them will surely come into my life for life; I have God's Word on that!

In His will,

Lady Ivy

Bibliography

Macartney, Clarence Edward. Great Women of the Bible. Kregal Publications, Grand Rapids, Mi:1992.

Smith, William. Nelson's Quick Reference Bible Dictionary. Thomas Nelson Publishers, Nashville: 1993.

Patterson, R.F. ed. The New Webster's Expanded Dictionary. P.S.I. & Assoc., Miami: 1991.

Unger, Merrill F. & William White Jr. Vine's Complete Expository Dictionary of Old and New Testament Words. Thomas Nelson Publishers, Nashville: 1996.

Bovo, Mary Jane. The Family Pregnancy: A Revolutionary 12-month Houlistic and Medical Guide to Maternity. Donald I. Fine, Inc. New York: 1994.

Jackson, Frank. Practical Housebuilding for Practically Everyone. McGraw Hill Book Company. New York: 1985.

Zeis, Cecy. Spiritual Warfare. Class Notes. World Harvest Bible College, Dominion Hall. Fall 1999.

Hayford, Jack W. (ed). Spirit Filled Life Bible for Students. Thomas Nelson Publishers. Nashville, 1995

Vine, W.E. Vine's Complete Expository Dictionary of Old and New Testament Words. Merrill F. Unger and William White Jr., ed. Thomas Nelson Publishers. Nashville: 1996.

If this book has been a blessing to you,
Please send your comments to
Jehovah Shammah Ministries
Lady Ivy A. Ashley
jehovahshammah07@hotmail.com or
ladyiashley@yahoo.com
Please include your prayer request.

Printed in the United States
20614LVS00001B/277

9 781413 439892